The Bible in Political Debate

The Bible in Political Debate

What Does It Really Say?

Edited by
Frances Flannery and Rodney A. Werline

Bloomsbury T&T Clark
An imprint of Bloomsbury Publishing Plc

B L O O M S B U R Y
LONDON • OXFORD • NEW YORK • NEW DELHI • SYDNEY

Bloomsbury T&T Clark

An imprint of Bloomsbury Publishing Plc

Imprint previously known as T&T Clark

50 Bedford Square	1385 Broadway
London	New York
WC1B 3DP	NY 10018
UK	USA

www.bloomsbury.com

**BLOOMSBURY, T&T CLARK and the Diana logo are trademarks of
Bloomsbury Publishing Plc**

First published 2016

British Library Cataloguing-in-Publication Data
A catalogue record for this book is available from the British Library.

ISBN:	HB:	978-0-5676-6661-1
	PB:	978-0-5676-6657-4
	ePDF:	978-0-5676-6658-1
	ePub:	978-0-5676-6659-8

Library of Congress Cataloging-in-Publication Data
A catalog record for this book is available from the Library of Congress.

Cover design: Nick Evans
Cover image © Shutterstock

Typeset by Integra Software Services Pvt. Ltd.

For S. and H. – ff

For D. and L. – rw

CONTENTS

CONTRIBUTORS

Hector Avalos, Ph.D., is Professor of Religious Studies at Iowa State University, Ames, IA, USA.

Kelley Coblentz Bautch, Ph.D., is Associate Professor of Religious Studies at St. Edward's University, Austin, TX, USA.

Daniel K. Falk, Ph.D., is Professor of Classics and Ancient Mediterranean Studies and Chaiken Family Chair in Jewish Studies at the Pennsylvania State University, University Park, PA, USA.

Frances Flannery, Ph.D., is Professor of Religion and Director of the Center for the Interdisciplinary Study of Terrorism and Peace at James Madison University, Harrisonburg, VA, USA.

Jonathan L. Jackson, M.T.S., M.S., is a Ph.D. Candidate in Cultural Anthropology at the Maxwell School of Citizenship and Public Affairs, Syracuse University, Syracuse, NY, USA.

Andrew Klumpp, M.Div., is a Ph.D. Student in Religious Studies at Southern Methodist University, Dallas, TX, USA.

John F. Kutsko, Ph.D., is Executive Director of the Society of Biblical Literature and Affiliated Faculty at Candler School of Theology, Emory University, Atlanta, GA, USA.

Bert Jan Lietaert Peerbolte, Ph.D., is Professor of New Testament Studies at Vrije Universiteit Amsterdam, the Netherlands; President of the Dutch Research School for Theology and Religious Studies (NOSTER); and Fellow at the Forschungszentrum für internationale und interdisziplinäre Theologie, Universität Heidelberg, Germany.

Jack Levison, Ph.D., is W. J. A. Power Professor of Old Testament Interpretation and Biblical Hebrew at Southern Methodist University, Perkins School of Theology, Dallas, TX, USA.

Judith H. Newman, Ph.D., is Associate Professor of Hebrew Bible and Early Judaism, Emmanuel College of Victoria University in the University of Toronto, Toronto, ON, Canada.

Emerson B. Powery, Ph.D., is Professor of Biblical Studies and Coordinator of Ethnic & Area Studies at Messiah College, Mechanicsburg, PA, USA.

Christopher A. Rollston, Ph.D., is Professor of Northwest Semitic Languages and Literatures, Department of Classical and Near Eastern Languages and Civilizations, George Washington University, Washington, D.C., USA.

Colleen Shantz, Ph.D., is Associate Professor, Faculty of Theology, St. Michael's College. She is cross-appointed to Department for the Study of Religion in the University of Toronto, Toronto, ON, Canada.

Rodney A. Werline, Ph.D., is Professor of Religious Studies and the Leman and Marie Barnhill Endowed Chair in Religious Studies at Barton College, Wilson, NC, USA. He is also the director of the Barton College Center for Religious Studies.

ACKNOWLEDGMENTS

A work like this is the product of many hands, minds, and hearts.

We are extremely grateful to the authors of these chapters—accomplished biblical scholars who were willing to write for a new public audience. Most of us have not written much for that audience, but we were motivated by care for the public square and concern about what is happening in public discourse in the United States and the world. It was such a pleasure talking about current issues among ourselves and a distinct honor to share it with our readers.

We are very grateful to T&T Clark/Bloomsbury Press. Our editor Dominic Mattos recognized the uniqueness and merits of this volume immediately and his enthusiasm helped push this project to completion. Miriam Cantwell, our supportive editorial assistant, has helped at every step of the way. We owe much thanks to John Kutsko, Executive Director of the Society of Biblical Literature (SBL), who not only wrote the conclusion to this volume, but who also brings to the SBL the wider call to public engagement that we are attempting in this project. Many thanks also go to our meticulous and helpful copy editor Anna Kelleher. Our student intern, Emily Cannon, supported us in early stages with valuable research.

We aimed to strike a more accessible tone in this volume than in our usual scholarship, which meant omitting the seemingly endless collection of footnotes that documents our evidence and sources. Each of us in the volume, however, most definitely builds on the work of the biblical scholars who have gone before us and who have taught us.

We would like to thank our readers, who desire to think openly and critically about these issues and who wish to inject thoughtful, respectful debate into our communities and policy debates.

Most of all, Frances and Rod would like to thank our families for their continual support of yet another project together that began with a phone call and the sentences, "Hey—I think I've got a pretty good idea! What do you think?"

—Frances Flannery, Ph.D. (Harrisonburg, VA) and
Rodney A. Werline, Ph.D. (Wilson, NC), March 30, 2016

ABBREVIATIONS

BBC	British Broadcasting Company
B.C.E.	Before the Common Era, the period also known as "B.C.," before the year "0"
C.E.	The Common Era, the period also known as "A.D.," after the year "0"
Col.	Colossians, a book in the New Testament
1 Cor.	First Corinthians, a book in the New Testament
2 Cor.	Second Corinthians, a book in the New Testament
Deut.	Deuteronomy, the fifth book in the Jewish Tanakh or Christian Old Testament
Eph.	Ephesians, a book in the New Testament
Gal.	Galatians, a book in the New Testament
Gen.	Genesis, the first book of the Jewish and Christian Bibles
Heb.	Hebrews, a book in the New Testament
Isa.	Isaiah, a book in the Jewish Tanakh or Christian Old Testament
JCCC	Jewish Climate Change Campaign
Jer.	Jeremiah, a book in the Jewish Tanakh or Christian Old Testament
JPS	Jewish Publication Society Tanakh or Hebrew Bible

2 Kgs.	2 Kings, a book in the Jewish Tanakh or Christian Old Testament
KJV	King James Version of the Bible, Old and New Testaments
Lev.	Leviticus, a book in the Jewish Tanakh or Christian Old Testament
Matt.	The Gospel according to Matthew, a book in the New Testament
m.Nid.	The tractate Niddah in the Mishnah, a Jewish law code from about 200 C.E.
m.Ohol.	The tractate Oholot in the Mishnah, a Jewish law code from about 200 C.E.
NRSV	New Revised Standard Version of the Bible, Old and New Testaments
Num.	Numbers, a book in the Jewish Tanakh or Christian Old Testament
1 Pet.	1 Peter, a book in the New Testament
Phil.	Philippians, a book in the New Testament
Phlm.	Philemon, a book in the New Testament
PRRI	Public Religion Research Institute
Ps.	Psalms, a book in the Jewish Tanakh or Christian Old Testament
Rev.	The Book of Revelation, the last book in the New Testament
Rom.	Romans, a book in the New Testament
RSV	Revised Standard Version of the Bible, Old and New Testaments
1 Tim.	Timothy, a book in the New Testament
UNHCR	United Nations High Commissioner on Refugees

Introduction

Frances Flannery and Rodney A. Werline

On a wet and muddy March 4, 1865, Abraham Lincoln stood outside the Capitol Building before an enthusiastic crowd. This was the inauguration ceremony for his second term as president (Donald 1995). While the Civil War still hung in the balance, the tide had turned in favor of the Union armies. In a few weeks, Richmond would fall to General Ulysses S. Grant, and within another week, General Robert E. Lee would surrender to Grant at Appomattox Courthouse, Virginia. Tragically, within a week from that news, John Wilkes Booth would assassinate Lincoln.

On that second inauguration day, however, Lincoln delivered perhaps his best speech next to the Gettysburg Address. This speech was brief and lacking in specific policies or an agenda for his second term. Instead, Lincoln leveled a grim assessment of the past four years in which he seemed to lay the blame for the war at everyone's feet, holding the North along with the South as guilty of benefiting from slavery (Donald 1995). As the president mused over the religious activities of both North and South, he highlighted the role of the Bible in contributing to the conflicting views on slavery and the war: "Both read the same Bible, and pray to the same God, and each invokes His aid against the other" (Basler 1946).

Indeed, both sides had read the same Bible and found within it justification for their positions. Slaves routinely had to endure white preachers admonishing them with Ephesians 6:5: "Slaves obey your masters." Northern abolitionist preachers and authors argued that slavery violated the Bible's teaching that all humans are created in the image of God and that the institution completely contradicted the Gospel of Christ (Gaustad and Schmidt 2002).

Lincoln's position also was not without biblical justification. He declared that the war had come upon the nation as a whole as God's punishment for slavery, a position others shared: "The prayers of both [sides] could not be answered; that of neither has been answered fully. The Almighty has his own purposes" (Basler 1946). Lincoln questions those who use the Bible to claim that God is on their side. Ironically, he does this by quoting Matthew 18:7 (parallel Luke 17:1):

> "Woe unto the world because of offences! for [*sic*] it must needs be that offences come; but woe to that man by whom the offence cometh!" If we shall suppose that American Slavery is one of those offences which, in the providence of God, must needs come, but which…He now wills to remove, and that he gives to both North and South, this terrible war,…shall we discern therein any departure from those divine attributes which the believers in a Living God always ascribe to him? (Basler 1946)

Before Lincoln closes his speech, he includes another quote from the Bible to support his position: "[T]he judgments of the Lord, are true and righteous altogether." These words come from Psalm 19:9. Thus, this one speech contains three different perspectives that claim to be based on the Bible.

Americans have a complicated relationship with the Bible. In some ways, this may relate to competing images we hold dear from our shared national past. First, Americans have seized on the image of the Puritan New England colony established for freedom of religion as the American ideal. When people invoke this image, however, they often do so to claim that persecuted people came here to found a specifically Christian land. From that colonial setting also arose the words of John Winthrop, Governor of the Massachusetts Bay colony: "[W]e shall be as a city on a hill" (Gaustad and Schmidt 2002). These words, applied here to the Massachusetts colonists, come from Jesus's ideal for the disciples in the Sermon on the Mount (Matt. 5:14). Since Winthrop said those words, the biblical phrase has been repeated over and over in American political speeches, especially in the twentieth century, to allude to America as a Christian nation and to tout American exceptionalism.

The second image arises from James Madison and Thomas Jefferson's firm dedication to establishing the separation of church and state. Their efforts are most visible in Madison's Memorial and Remonstrance against Religious Assessments (1785), with which he successfully defeated Patrick Henry's legislative proposal to levy a tax that would benefit Virginia religious schools, Jefferson's Virginia Statute on Religious Freedom (1786), which Madison shepherded through the state legislature, and the First Amendment of the Bill of Rights (1791). That Amendment states: "Congress shall make no law respecting an establishment of religion, or prohibiting the free exercise thereof." According to Jefferson's *Letter to the Danbury Baptists* in 1802, the First Amendment had established a "wall of separation" between church and state. Madison too maintained belief in a strong separation between church and state. In his later years, he worried about any action that may have transgressed the line of separation, including days of prayer and fasting that he declared as president (Broadwater 2012). The Constitution, in Article VI, had also declared that no religious test could be required to hold public office. While several years passed before all states complied, this was nevertheless the law of the land (Gaustad and Schmidt 2002).

The Bible in contemporary American political debate

Throughout the complicated history of the United States, two attitudes have become firmly rooted in the American imagination. On the one hand, America is the biblical "city on a hill" founded as a Christian land. On the other hand, America is the nation that ensures a separation of church and state that protects individual freedom of and from religion. Given this firmly rooted conflicted national self-identity, it is not surprising to hear American politicians embrace one image or the other. They may even attempt to hold onto both at the same time. On both sides of the aisle and at every level of political life, political officials, party representatives, and pundits employ biblical imagery, allusions to biblical texts, and explicit quotations from the Bible as support for public policy. The issues are as far-ranging as abortion, the death penalty, self-determined euthanasia, school education, taxation, welfare, climate change, marriage, adoption, gun control, war, and immigration.

On a national level, the Bible is invoked as an authority in presidential, judicial, and legislative contexts alike. The very swearing in of each president includes an oath of office that ends "so help me God," uttered with one hand on the Bible—or maybe on two Bibles, as in the inaugurations of Truman, Eisenhower, Nixon, and Obama.

Presidents sometimes use the Bible to argue for particular policies. In a public speech in 2014, President Obama openly appealed to the authority of Exodus 23 in order to explain his position on immigration, declaring: "Scripture tells us that we shall not oppress a stranger, for we know the heart of a stranger—we were once strangers too" (Obama 2014). Again, in his January 2016 speech on his executive action on gun control, he told the moving story of Zaevion Dobson, a fifteen-year-old who was shot while protecting his friends. Afterward, President Obama cited Jesus's words from John 15:13, "Greater love hath no man than this that a man lay down his life for his friends" (Obama 2016). He then concluded that, while we may not be as courageous as Zaevion, we can vote out of office those politicians who reject gun safety reform measures.

In appealing to biblical words as his moral authority, President Obama was not out of step with other recent presidents. President Reagan designated 1983 as the "Year of Bible" through Proclamation 5018 after speaking at the National Prayer Breakfast and saying of the Bible: "Inside its pages lie all the answers to all the problems man has ever known" (Reagan 1983a; 1983b). Reagan was in fact authorized to take this step by Congress, which had already approved 1983 as the "Year of the Bible" on October 4, 1982, by Public Law 97–280 (Senate Joint Resolution 165), 96 Stat. 1211 (97th Congress 1982).

Within the Capitol Building, the prominence of the Bible appears as a constant reminder etched in stone. In the relief portraits over the gallery doors of the House Chamber are the side-face profiles of twenty-two lawgivers, including Hammurabi, Solon, and Napoleon I, which are all oriented toward the centrally located, full face of Moses, the receiver of biblical law. Israeli Prime Minister Benyamin Netanyahu noted the centrality of the sculpture of Moses in his 2015 speech to Congress when he declared, "Facing me right up there in the gallery, overlooking all of us … is the image of Moses … Moses led our people from slavery to the gates of the Promised Land." In this speech taking firm stances against Iran and ISIS, Netanyahu then directly quoted from Deuteronomy 31:6 in the original Hebrew: "Be strong and resolute, neither fear nor dread them" (Netanyahu 2015). In a historic speech in 2015, Pope Francis also addressed a Joint Session of Congress, reminding lawmakers "Moses…the lawgiver of the people of Israel symbolizes the need of peoples to keep alive their sense of unity by means of just legislation" (Pope Francis 2015).

Showing dedication to the Bible is often a prerequisite for successful political life in the United States, and some cultural critics wonder whether anyone could now be president without claiming to be Christian. In the run-up to the 2016 presidential election, both Democrat and Republican hopefuls talked about the influence of the Bible on their lives. In 2014, Hillary Rodham Clinton stated in an interview: "The Bible was and remains the biggest influence on my thinking. I was raised reading it, memorizing passages from it and being guided by it. I still find it a source of wisdom, comfort and encouragement" (Hillary Rodham Clinton 2014). Democratic presidential hopeful Bernie Sanders likewise appealed to the authority of the Bible when addressing an audience at the conservative Christian Liberty University in Lynchburg, Virginia, in 2015. To support his policies aimed at helping the poor, Sanders quoted from Matthew 7:12 and Amos 5:24. However, Sanders—who self-identifies as culturally Jewish—explained his use of the Bible in an interfaith context, saying, "I am motivated by a vision which exists in all of the great religions—in Christianity, in Judaism, in Islam, Buddhism and other religions—and which is so beautifully and clearly stated in Matthew 7:12" (Markoe 2015).

On the Republican side, the presidential candidates for 2016 were willing to connect an explicitly Christian interpretation of the Bible with their stated public policy positions. Republican contenders Ben Carson, Ted Cruz, Mike Huckabee, Bobby Jindal, and Donald Trump all sought to connect their policy positions to the Bible. Sometimes the physical biblical book itself functioned as symbol, as when Trump waved around a Bible while speaking to an audience of evangelicals (Morrongiello 2015). In the second Republican presidential debate, candidate Carson explained his flat tax proposal as a biblical "tithe," which originates with biblical agricultural contributions to the Temple and its staff (Lev. 27:30–33; Num. 18:21–28; Republican Presidential Debate 2015). Huckabee, a former Southern Baptist minister, clearly linked his positions against same-sex marriage and abortion to the Bible, stating about the former, "And as a biblical issue—unless I get a new version of the Scriptures, it's not really my place to say, 'OK, I'm going to evolve'" (Martin 2015).

State government has also witnessed explicit appeals to biblical authority. Perhaps the zenith occurred in 2011 with then-Texas Governor Rick Perry's public call to repentance at the evangelical Christian rally "The Response," a gathering that was meant to end Texas' drought through prayer, fasting, and dedication to Jesus, based on an interpretation of Joel 2. Over 30,000 people showed up at Reliant Stadium, answering "a call for prayer for a nation at the crossroads" (Response 2015).

However, it is in local government that the Bible maintains its greatest political influence, often barely skirting the legal separation of church and state. As one example among many, in Rockingham County, Virginia, students in public school may voluntarily engage in Bible study during school hours in "Virginia's Weekly Religion Education," a program run by "self-governing local councils" claiming to conduct "a biblically sound Christian curriculum that uses the Bible as its primary text." To ensure legality, the classes are provided in buildings near or adjacent to the school property line (Weekday Religious Education 2012). In fact, the Supreme Court seemingly affirmed this blurring of the line between church and state at the local level as a result of its 2014 decision in *Town of Greece v. Galloway*. By a 5–4 vote, the court ruled that local governments may begin meetings with prayer because it is a long-standing American tradition.

The Bible is revered not only by small town councils, but by large cities as well. In 2009, the National Bible Association chose Philadelphia as the "National Bible City of 2009." An official city proclamation, signed by the president of the City Council of Philadelphia Anna Verna, accepted the designation and declared November 22–28, 2009 as "Bible Week" since "the Bible has been a historic source of moral strength and spiritual guidance for many people throughout the history of Philadelphia" (City Council 2009).

The Bible according to biblical literalists

Each of these political examples assumes that the meaning of the biblical text is well known, undebatable, and a proper source for moral and political decision-making. Some politicians or pundits even believe in the "literal" interpretation of the Bible, which maintains that it is "literally" true and "inerrant" or without mistake.

Problems with the literal approach to biblical interpretation abound, however. To begin, which translation of the Bible would be literally true? The King James Version, which only relies on late tenth-century manuscripts? We now have manuscripts that are 1,000 years older and thus most likely much more reliable. Or perhaps it is the Revised Standard Version, New International Version, or New American Standard Version of the Bible that is literally true? Since these are English translations of the ancient languages of the Bible—Hebrew and Aramaic for the Hebrew Bible or Christian Old Testament and Greek for the New Testament—they are each an *interpretation*. Upon close reading, there are significant differences among these English translations, not to mention among modern translations in French, German, Japanese, and so forth. Which ones are literally true? They don't always agree with one another.

If we search for the earliest available manuscripts of the books of the Bible in their original languages, we find that we lack a whole copy of the New Testament until the fourth century. The earliest version of the Hebrew Bible that we have—the ancient library called the Dead Sea Scrolls—doesn't set off the books in today's "Bible" as a separate collection.

Also, there are serious differences among the existing early versions of the New Testament that we do have. Taking all the earliest Greek manuscripts of the New Testament together and some early (pre-sixth-century) translations into other languages—such as Syriac, Coptic, and Ethiopic—produces over 100,000 meaningful variations. A team of translators has to decide on all of these choices before they ever appear in an English (or other) translation, often erasing these editorial decisions altogether. Which ones are literally true?

Then, even if we *were* to find the perfect original manuscript of all the books of the Bible, we would find that interpretation is still a problem, since there are contradictions among the books too numerous to mention here. That is why from the earliest periods, Jewish interpreters accepted at minimum four levels of interpretation: a plain meaning, a metaphorical meaning, an inter-textual meaning that looked for cross references to other sacred Jewish books, and a mystical meaning. The Talmud—a fifth-century

C.E. Jewish book that holds sacred status in Judaism only second
to the Hebrew Bible—concluded in one story that there were at
least 613 interpretations of *every letter* of the Torah. While this is
perhaps an overexaggeration, it gets to the point that even while the
"literal" or "plain" meaning may be accepted, it stands alongside or
in tension with other meanings.

The leaders and teachers of the earliest Christian Church
likewise often avoided a "literal" interpretation of the Bible in favor
of understanding it as allegory, moral teaching, or a mystical text.
Bishop Papias, a Church leader speaking in the late first century
to early second century C.E., even warned against trusting books
written about Jesus. Although he liked "Mark" he cautioned
against thinking it was an exact chronology of what happened.
Instead, the Christian Bishop urged fellow Christians to find
someone who had known Jesus or who had known someone else
who had. From the Middle Ages to the modern age, interpreters
such as Martin Luther viewed biblical passages as allegory—
metaphors to be interpreted in a variety of ways. This approach was
the preferred method, viewed as the deeper meaning of scripture.

"Taking the Bible to be literally true" as *the only way to
interpret the Bible* is actually a largely American Protestant
phenomenon that is only a little over 100 years old. It arose in
the Fundamentalist Christian platform of 1911 to combat forms
of Christianity that were updating their theologies in relation
to the modern world. It presumes that the plain meaning of
the Bible that interpreters will find is in perfect alignment with
fundamentalist doctrines, which are often unclear to those who
are not fundamentalist Christians.

The Bible according to critical biblical scholars

Experts on the Bible—scholars who study the Bible as a
profession—have rarely weighed in as a group on the use of the
Bible in deciding public policy matters. Too often, we have kept
our knowledge to ourselves. Biblical scholars have studied the
biblical texts extremely carefully, typically in the original languages
in which the Bible was written and copied. With rigor, we have

studied the ancient historical settings in which the Bible was written, including the societies of the ancient Near East, Greece, and Rome that influenced the authors of the various biblical books. However, in large part due to our lack of public outreach, the public is often unaware of the conclusions of biblical scholars regarding the passages frequently cited by politicians. Despite the publication of some more popular books by biblical scholars in the last two decades and excellent reflections on religion and politics written by scholars of religion, *biblical scholars* have not written much for the general population on the use of the Bible in political debate.[1] This book seeks to address that gap.

In general, biblical scholars are a bit of a mystery to members of the general public. Some see us as atheists driven to disprove the historical and spiritual meaning of the Bible, while others see us as pastors, rabbis, or Sunday school teachers who want to preach the message of the Bible. Some dismiss our academic understandings as competing against the inspired positions of their faith traditions. A few view us as curious, pipe smoking professors obsessed with arcane languages, perhaps hiding the Dead Sea Scrolls in a conspiracy to hoard our knowledge for ourselves. There are also those who picture us going on the occasional wild adventure like Indiana Jones. Even our academic colleagues from other disciplines sometimes confuse us with theologians, who interpret the Bible from the perspective of particular faith traditions.

The truth is that biblical scholars are people, and people vary. Some of us match some aspects of the descriptions above, but there is no "type" of person who is a biblical scholar. What we all have in common is a lengthy training of a decade or much longer that evaluates the meaning of a biblical text within its ancient setting by using well-established methods. Biblical scholars tend to ask questions such as, "What did the Bible say in its original context?" and "How was the Bible interpreted by a certain culture in a particular historical period?" In fact, as the essay near the end of this book by Coblentz Bautch makes clear, there are different Bibles for various religions and denominations and the books of the Bible were not originally composed together or as a sacred text.

Biblical scholars employ a number of methods to read and interpret the Bible. Perhaps the most basic method of biblical scholarship is "literary criticism," which entails reading the text extremely carefully in its original languages. This might illuminate problems within the text itself, which may necessitate reconstructions from several manuscripts, given that we don't have the original texts of the Bible. Biblical scholars also use a method called "historical criticism" that evaluates a text in the context of its society at the time of composition, especially other traditions with which the biblical authors would have been familiar. By knowing how the authors of Genesis changed the traditional story, readers of the Bible can better grasp what the biblical authors meant to relay as important.

To illustrate historical criticism with a non-sacred example, consider the story *Goldilocks and the Three Bears*. If we were to tell the story but conclude by saying that Goldilocks shoots the bears when they return home, an adult audience would be likely to laugh in surprise, perhaps exclaiming, "That's not how it goes!" They would recognize immediately the innovation that is supposed to draw our attention. Yet if we did not know how the story was "supposed" to go, wouldn't it be just as *reasonable, rational, and logical* to ask, "How are there talking bears? Did they build this house themselves? What is this strange porridge that is hot in one bowl, cold in another, and a medium temperature in the third? Is it some kind of magical porridge?" These questions are "reasonable" for anyone who does not know *Goldilocks*, but they are silly for anyone who does.

Similarly, historical criticism helps us avoid getting stuck with such questions when reading the Bible because we know "how the story goes." A reasonable but fruitless question would be, "What are the waters that are separated from the waters in Genesis 1?" That phrasing is very strange in modern English. The answer from historical criticism is simple: many ancient Near Eastern peoples believed that at the creation of the world there was already water everywhere, which was gathered, divided, or held back as an early step of creation. This is not a novel point to which the author of Genesis 1 is attempting to draw our attention—it is just "how the story goes." However, contrasting Genesis 1 with Mesopotamian creation stories reveals that Genesis' repeated declaration that creation is "good" *is* an important development. Historical criticism helps us in our effort to read the Bible in the way that the ancient author likely intended it to be heard.

Aims of this book

The contributors to this book are all professional biblical scholars who are extremely well-versed in the original languages, texts, archaeology, and historical settings of the Bible. For the purposes of this project, we use the Hebrew Bible/Old Testament and New Testament as it has been translated into English in the New Revised Standard Version of the Bible, unless an author notes the use of a different translation.

In Part One, each author has taken up a contemporary political issue for which the Bible has frequently been invoked in public debate. Sometimes, as in the case of the first essay on "family values," specific biblical verses aren't explicitly mentioned in support of the issue, but public perception assumes that the Bible supports one political position over another. In other cases, politicians or pundits have cited particular biblical verses in support of a policy stance. The authors in this section of the volume turn to the Bible to ask, *What did the Bible say about this issue in its original context?*—an approach known as literary–historical criticism. Part Two provides a historical perspective on how the Bible was interpreted in the setting of debates on the expulsion of the First Nations in early North American colonial history, slavery, and women's rights. The primary question these authors ask is, *How was the Bible interpreted in this period in relation to this public policy?* Finally, Part Three reflects back on this project with two essays. One explains how the texts now known as the Bible came to be collected as a canon of Scripture, that is, as authoritative, sacred text. The last essay in this volume suggests that biblical scholarship shows compromise to be a biblical ethic, an observation with tremendous importance for our current political climate.

The approach taken in this book strives to be nonpartisan. Each individual contributor may or may not like the position that the Bible provides on his or her particular issue. As citizens, we may feel strongly in favor of one position over another in public policy debates. However, as authors we have each striven *not* to let our positions on public policy issues influence our interpretations of the text's original meaning. We have firmly kept in mind that our job is not to "rescue" the biblical text from its premodern and occasionally harsh positions.

The demographics of the contributors to this volume differ. Some of us are persons of faith in particular traditions, including Jews, Catholics, Protestants, and Buddhists. Other contributors view themselves as nonreligious or openly identify as atheists, secular, or agnostic. Some of us are pastors; some of us avoid religious settings of worship. There are men as well as women, older and younger scholars, and scholars from the United States, Canada, and the Netherlands, representing a variety of ethnic and national heritages. Some of us are immigrants or the children of immigrants, some of us are differently abled, and we embrace differing sexual identities. The contributors include both conservatives and liberals, and the authors do not write with intent to support the positions of any political parties.

This book aims to be more publicly accessible than much of our typical biblical scholarship. Yet, each of us builds on the work of all the scholars who have gone before us, and we would be remiss in not noting that what is represented here is also a sample of the vibrant academic conversations that transpire in conferences. The best of this scholarship is evident in the Society of Biblical Literature, the professional society of our discipline.

While each essay represents a sterling example of biblical scholarship, it is never meant to be the final word on the matter. Rather, this book seeks to encourage further lively exploration of the meaning of these biblical texts using the tools of biblical scholarship. This is especially the case in relation to the public policy issues for which the Bible is so often cited by politicians and pundits.

Although we as scholars strive to be objective interpreters of biblical texts, studies in the humanities and social sciences have taught us that there can never be a wholly objective, non-biased interpretation. Even as academics, each of us is a product of our environment and culture. Our personal histories, social locations, and political positions can bleed into our interpretations without our knowing it. Also, as scholars, we sometimes disagree with one another. However, each scholar must make her or his point based on the standards of biblical scholarship. We do not make claims based on inspiration, revelation, or memory of a text, but rather on a careful reading of the text in its social context.

Hence, the differences between our approach as biblical scholars and that of the politicians cited in this volume are significant.

As biblical scholars we are aware of the range of possible interpretations of biblical texts. We strive to be self-aware of the biases that can influence our interpretations. We don't make the text say what we want it to say, even if the text makes us uncomfortable.

Much of the time, the contributors to this volume conclude that the Bible does not speak directly to the policy issues on which it is invoked, since the biblical authors knew nothing of climate change caused by humans, same-sex marriage, or medical abortion. Even when biblical authors address issues familiar to us, such as slavery, marriage, poverty, work, the status of women, and submission to governments, it is in very different historical and social settings from our own. Also, as some of the essays in this book note, the Bible can be construed as having very different answers in relation to a particular policy, depending on which passages one reads. This raises important questions about the ways in which politicians and pundits uncritically assume an understanding of the Bible without exhibiting awareness of how they have arrived at those particular interpretations.

Overall, *The Bible in Political Debate* brings biblical scholarship into the discussion of certain biblical texts that are "cherry-picked" by politicians and pundits for their policy positions. By using the tools of mainstream modern biblical scholarship, each contributor to this volume has striven to provide as unbiased a reading of the Bible as is possible. After hearing our perspectives, it is for the readers themselves to decide what the texts mean to them. It is for individual readers and our society to decide in what ways—or whether—the Bible should serve as a basis for forming public policy.

Works Cited

97th Congress. Joint Resolution, Public Law 97–280. October 4, 1982. https://www.gpo.gov/fdsys/pkg/STATUTE-96/pdf/STATUTE-96 -Pg1211.pdf (accessed January 10, 2016).

Basler, Roy P. (ed.). *Abraham Lincoln: His Speeches and Writings*. New York: De Capo, 1946.

Broadwater, Jeff. *James Madison: A Son of Virginia & a Founder of the Nation*. Chapel Hill, NC: The University of North Carolina Press, 2012.

Chancey, Mark A., Carol Meyers and Eric M. Meyers (eds.). *The Bible in the Public Square: Its Enduring Influence in American Life*. Atlanta: Society of Biblical Literature Press, 2014.

City Council of Philadelphia. "A Proclamation." *National Bible Association: Welcome to National Bible City*. 2009. http://biblecity .org/citycouncilproclamation (accessed January 10, 2016).

Clinton, Hillary Rodham. "Hillary Rodham Clinton: By the Book." *New York Times Sunday Book Review*. June 11, 2014. http://www .nytimes.com/2014/06/15/books/review/hillary-rodham-clinton-bythe -book.html?ref=review&_r=2 (accessed January 12, 2016).

Donald, David Herbert. *Lincoln*. New York: Simon & Schuster, 1995.

Gaustad, Edwin S. and Leigh E. Schmidt. *The Religious History of America*. San Francisco: Harper, 2002.

Getto, Erica and Kavish Harjal. "8 Times that a 10 Commandments Monument Had Its Day in Court." July 8, 2015. http://www.msnbc .com/msnbc/8-times-10-commandments-monument-had-its-day-court (accessed January 3, 2016).

Markoe, Lauren. "5 Faith Facts about Bernie Sanders: Unabashedly Irreligious." *Religion News Service*. September 22, 2015. http:// www.religionnews.com/2015/09/22/5-faith-facts-bernie-sanders -unabashedly-irreligious/ (accessed February 8, 2016).

Martin, Samuel. "6 Interesting Facts about Mike Huckabee's Christian Faith." *Christian Post Politics*. May 11, 2015. http://www.msnbc.com/ msnbc/8-times-10-commandments-monument-had-its-day-court

Morrongiello, Gabby. "Trump Waves Copy of 'Favorite Book' the Bible." *The Washington Examiner*. September 25, 2015. http://www .washingtonexaminer.com/trump-waves-copy-of-favorite-book-the -bible/article/2572830 (accessed January 2, 2016).

Netanyahu, Benjamin. "The Complete Transcript of Netanyahu's Address to Congress." *Washington Post*. March 3, 2015. https://www .washingtonpost.com/news/post-politics/wp/2015/03/03/full-text -netanyahus-address-to-congress/ (accessed January 2, 2016).

Obama, Barack. The White House, Office of the Press Secretary. "Remarks by the President in Address to the Nation on Immigration." November 20, 2014. https://www.whitehouse.gov/the-press -office/2014/11/20/remarks-president-address-nation-immigration (accessed January 6, 2016).

Obama, Barack. The White House, Office of the Press Secretary. "Remarks by the Present on Common-Sense Gun Safety Reform." January 5, 2016. https://www.whitehouse.gov/the-press -office/2016/01/05/remarks-president-common-sense-gun-safety -reform (accessed Jan.10, 2016).

Pope Francis. Address to Joint Meeting of Congress. September 24, 2015. http://www.c-span.org/video/?328063-1/pope-francis-address-joint -meeting-congress (accessed February 11, 2016).

Reagan, Ronald. Remarks at the Annual National Prayer Breakfast. February 3, 1983a. http://www.reagan.utexas.edu/archives/speeches/1983/20383a.htm (accessed March 10, 2016).

Reagan, Ronald. Proclamation 5018—Year of the Bible 1983. February 3, 1983b. http://www.reagan.utexas.edu/archives/speeches/1983/20383b.htm (accessed November 15, 2015).

Republican Presidential Debate. Transcript. *New York Times*. November 11, 2015. http://www.nytimes.com/2015/11/11/us/politics/transcript-republican-presidential-debate.html?_r=0 (accessed November 15, 2016).

The Response. 2015. http://theresponseusa.com/ (September 22, 2015).

Weekday Religious Education. March 17, 2012. http://virginiawre.blogspot.com/ (March 20, 2016).

PART ONE

The Bible in Contemporary Political Debate

1

The Bible and Family Values

Andrew Klumpp and Jack Levison

Forerunners and fledgling astronauts

On August 8, 1964, my parents give me a plastic astronaut helmet for my eighth birthday—with wings on the forehead and a small mouthpiece with wax paper, so that my voice sounds like I imagine it will on the moon. The lunar landing is still five years away—when my parents will wake me to watch, in the gray of our black and white television, real astronauts in real helmets landing on a real moon.

For now I am supremely happy. My father has a job in the city—he heads to Manhattan on the 7:15 train and returns on the 6:51. My mother cooks meatloaf on chilly autumn nights. I start little league this year and, as luck would have it, our team sponsor is Allied Candy Store.

I am the embodiment of family values: a breadwinner father and a stay-at-home mom. An elementary school I can walk to, with Brylcream—a little dab'll do ya'—fresh in my hair. A crush on my teacher, Miss Hamje, which tells me I'm straight. And Catholic families with hordes of kids—birth control is still taboo—as playmates.

Yes, I am the embodiment of family values, but, as I whisper into my astronaut mouthpiece, dreaming of moonscapes, I fail to realize that the ground, right here on earth, trembles under my feet.[1]

Just five weeks before my birthday, on July 2, 1964, the Civil Rights Act makes discrimination based on race, color, religion, sex, or national origin illegal. We are not in Mississippi or Alabama, but this great government act tweaks the familiarity of our world. Before this, and closer to home, Supreme Court decisions challenge values we have taken for granted. On the first day of summer vacation—June 25, 1962—the U.S. Supreme Court declares school-sponsored prayer unconstitutional in the landmark case, *Engel v. Vitale*. On June 17, 1963, during Mrs. Calzetta's second-grade class, the U.S. Supreme Court prohibits school officials from organizing prayers and devotional Bible readings in public schools in the controversial case, *Abington Township School District v. Schempp*. Public response is widespread and virulent. God, it is said, has been kicked out of schools (Dowland 2015). Fork Lane Elementary School puts me, and all of America with me, some argue, on the path to perdition.

Just twenty-three days before my eighth birthday—July 16, 1964—an off-duty police officer shoots fifteen-year-old James Powell in Harlem. Three weeks before my birthday, 8,000 African-Americans protest at the 28th precinct. The police press and shove; protesters react violently. The result? One dead. One hundred injured. Four hundred and fifty arrested.

But that is Manhattan, an island away. I am a Long Islander. I live on the terra firma of potato fields-turned suburbs.

Then the race riots spill over to the Bedford-Stuyvesant area of Brooklyn. We gape in horror at burning buildings, African-American fists thrust high in rage, and we begin to wonder. Bed-Stuy is twenty-seven miles from our home in Hicksville and only ten miles from my grandmother's apartment in Queens. The tremors come closer. The asphalt on which we play stickball at the schoolyard is not so solid any more.

Just six days before my birthday, half a world away, three North Vietnamese patrol boats attack the American destroyer U.S.S. Maddox. On August 4, news of the apparent attack escalates in the press, and President Lyndon B. Johnson retaliates with the first bombing of North Vietnam. With wild popular support, Congress passes the "Gulf of Tonkin Resolution," which allows the president "to take all necessary steps, including the use of armed force" to wage an undeclared war in Vietnam. Ocean swells in the Gulf of Tonkin will carry thousands of young men and women into the turmoil of protracted jungle battle.

By my eighth birthday, the world as we know it has changed. The values for which my family had fought in World War II— my father in the nose of a B-24 in Italy and my mother in a propeller factory in Pittsburgh—unravel. None of this keeps me from agonizing over strikeouts, staring mesmerized at men on the moon, or falling in love with a blonde-haired, blue-eyed Lutheran girl named Heidi, but all of it compacts to create unprecedented social revolution in the world into which I was born. And, just as influential, with this revolution comes a forceful grassroots backlash, an unparalleled effort to maintain the status quo, by Christians, evangelical and Catholic, committed to what would come famously to be known, if not well defined, as family values.

The quest for a messiah

Americans headed into the seventies with Vietnam in full swing, racial tensions at an all-time high, and devastating legal and legislative actions (not to mention hideous fashions and fads) on the horizon. Divorce rates soared. Women moved in droves into the workforce. Gays and lesbians, suspect since Senator Joseph McCarthy associated them with communism during the 1950s, gained momentum and public notoriety. The Equal Rights Amendment (ERA), which had languished for decades, picked up steam in Congress. The Supreme Court's 7–2 decision in *Roe v. Wade* forced the loosening of abortion laws in forty-six out of fifty states (Williams 2011).

The seventies were a decade of mobilization—transformation, even—for evangelical Christians. They began the decade disorganized but ended with virtual control of the Republican Party. It was a remarkable transition, with family values at its core. Congresswoman Phyllis Schlafly, Dr. James Dobson, the Reverend Jerry Falwell, and a slew of others would become household names in public American life.

Congresswoman and Harvard-educated Roman Catholic Phyllis Schlafly torpedoed the ERA in 1973–1974 by gathering a grassroots army of evangelical and Catholic women, who fought tooth and (manicured) nail against the feminist agenda of equal rights for women. Schlafly insisted that gender equality robbed women of their feminine mystique and made them vulnerable to the military draft (Williams 2011). The ERA would destroy the order of the family—and the order of the nation, where men go to work and war, while women stay home.

Slightly later, prominent evangelical child psychologist James Dobson worked to restore men to leadership in the family. This was not a political ruse. In 2004, Dobson recalled what God had said to him in the mid-seventies: "If this country is going to make it," God said to Dobson, "and if the family is going to survive, it will be because husbands and fathers begin to accept their responsibilities for leadership, and especially spiritual leadership in their own families ..." (Heltzel 2009). With the conviction of that call, Dobson began a ministry to men in 1976 and left Children's Hospital and the USC School of Medicine to found Focus on the Family in 1977 (Heltzel 2009).

One of the remarkable side effects of the seventies was an unholy alliance—or what a decade earlier had been deemed an unholy alliance—between Catholics and evangelicals. *Roe v. Wade*, in particular, forged this alliance. Catholics had long been opposed to abortion; evangelicals had not. The Southern Baptist Convention, in fact, in both 1971 and 1974, issued official statements that abortion was permissible in cases of incest, rape, mothers' health, and disabilities in fetuses (Williams 2011). For years, the dramatically increasing number of abortions had horrified many evangelicals, including pro-life Carl F. H. Henry, founder of the flagship evangelical magazine, *Christianity Today*, and the 1973 Roe ruling legalized their worst nightmare by making abortion, in their minds, a matter of convenience (Williams 2011).[2]

Christians bent on family values, however, needed more than a magazine and a jumble of organizations. They looked for a messiah, and one man fit the bill, down to the initials, J. C. A Sunday school teacher, born-again Christian, and family man with a likeable Southern drawl hit the campaign trail for the 1976 presidential election. Scandalized by skyrocketing divorce rates and out-of-wedlock births, Jimmy Carter, the embodiment of family values, even celebrated his thirtieth wedding anniversary on the campaign trail (Balmer 2011). With endorsements from Pentecostal televangelist Pat Robertson, Civil Rights activist Jesse Jackson, and a welter of other Christian leaders, Carter won the Democratic presidential nomination in 1976.

Carter's messianic reign was short-lived. Even during the campaign, his infamous *Playboy* interview, in which he confessed to lusting after women other than his wife Rosalynn, raised more than a few eyebrows (Balmer 2011). More damaging, he supported the ERA and waffled on abortion; personally opposed to abortion, he defended a woman's right to obtain one.

The real disaster occurred when Carter made good on his campaign promise to deal directly with family values. His White House Conference on Families in 1980 was a failure from the get-go, when he offended Catholics, in particular, by naming Patsy Fleming, a divorced mother of three, to lead the conference (Balmer 2011).[3] Even the word, "Families," troubled family values of Christians, who worried that the plural term *families* communicated the acceptance of more than the traditional family. Were single-parent and same-sex households included alongside the traditional American family?

Enter Jerry Falwell, a reluctant political figure, who had already answered that question for millions of Americans disillusioned by Carter's liberalism and the Democratic Party's secularism. Democrats had become the party of the feminist movement, the gay rights community, and the pro-choice agenda (Williams 2011). Falwell rallied a variety of Christian groups, founded an influential political organization called the Moral Majority, which championed family values, and condemned Jimmy Carter's conference.

With the full-throated approval of the Moral Majority and other grassroots movements, presidential candidate Ronald Reagan surged to the top of the Republican ticket. With open arms and an explicit family values agenda, Reagan welcomed Christians who felt scorned by Carter and the Democratic Party. The divorced governor of California assured them, "I know that you can't endorse me, but I want you to know that I endorse you and what you are doing" (Reagan 1980). In one fell swoop, family values' advocates found their new home in the Republican Party.

The 1980 party platforms tell the story of the politics of family values. The Republican Platform includes three straightforward statements on the "traditional family" and offers specific strategies for ways to protect the American ideal (Republican Party Platform 1980). The Democratic Platform includes a single ambiguous line: "The Democratic Party supports efforts to make federal programs more sensitive to the needs of the family, in all its diverse forms" (Democratic Party Platform 1980).[4] *Federal programs* and *diverse forms* did not appeal to family values' advocates.

Reagan won the 1980 election. Carter went home to Georgia.

In the end, advocates of family values did not win with the election of Reagan. Women would outnumber men on America's campuses and begin to dominate segments of the work force. Abortion would remain legal. Same-sex marriage would become legal. And Democrats would co-opt family values rhetoric. In 2004, presidential nominee John Kerry used family values to justify federal funding for social programs: "And it is time for those who talk about family values to start valuing families. You don't value families by kicking kids out of after school programs and taking cops off our streets, so that Enron can get another tax break. We believe in the family value of caring for our children and protecting the neighborhoods where they walk and play" (Kerry 2004). In 2014, President Barack Obama used family values to justify an executive order loosening immigration policies: "America's not a nation that should be tolerating the cruelty of ripping children from their parents' arms. We're a nation that values families, and we should work together to keep them together." The American Family Association decried Obama's appeal to family values on behalf of other nations' children (Wetzstein 2014).

No defense needed

The topic, *family values*, is a flexible umbrella term—imprecise, even—for which proponents offer precious little biblical evidence. References to family values are often relatively Bible free, for several reasons.

1   Family values wasn't so much the American Dream as an American Agenda—to shore up the family after the overindulgence of the twenties, the austerity of the thirties, the loss of men in the forties, and the threat of communist takeover in the fifties. The background of family values lies, then, not so much in recovering the imagined family of the biblical era, as in the ideal family of the 1950s, when veterans charged off to work and mothers tended the home, when Catholic homes burst at the seams with kids, when a neighborhood could be multiethnic, full of the sons and daughters of European immigrants, but not multiracial.

2   This imagined world came, if not to a screeching halt, at least to a visible slowdown during the 1960s and early 1970s. What suburban mothers and fathers needed was not so much a biblical basis for family as a *practical* way to control the heaving swells of change that took their daughters and sons to college and back home again with unconventional ideas and well-placed but trenchant postadolescent opposition to the Vietnam Conflict. The need for family values was existential. I know. My sister left in 1968 for Plattsburgh State University when I was heading into puberty. She returned with *The Harrad Experiment* and notions that upended my father's inherited conception of authority.

3   Most of the heavy Bible lifting had already happened in public discussion of individual social issues, such as abortion, same-sex relationships, pornography, and women's rights. As a catch-all term, then, *family values* hardly needed defending or attacking. That battle took place on the level of individual issues.

4   There is no need to launch a biblical defense of family values, the way one might wish to defend or attack gay marriage. Who imagines that traditional families are the enemy of the state? It is enough to say, as Hillary Clinton would in her campaign announcement, as late as June 2015: "[W]hen our families are strong, America is strong" (Clinton 2015). No need to appeal to the Bible. Family values are the apple pie of political rhetoric.

Digging down to the biblical bedrock of family values, therefore, is unnecessary on several counts. First, family values drew its inspiration less from the Bible than from the ideal, if unattainable, family after World War II. (Think *Leave It to Beaver*, which ran from October 4, 1957 until June 20, 1963.) Second, the real need in the defense of family values was existential, rooted in the need for parents to cope with the demands of a decade of unprecedented change. Third, the battle for the Bible took place on the level of individual issues, while *family values* was an umbrella term that encompassed all of them more generally. And fourth, family values could still—*can* still—be considered a self-evident truth: strong families lead to a strong America.

Families devalued

Still another reason why arguments for family values do not draw their inspiration from the Bible is the checkered view of family the Bible affords. For every text that supports the notion of a breadwinner father, a stay-at-home mom, and two well-scrubbed kids, there are dozens of biblical texts that attest to a very different experience of family values (Dowland 2015). In a real sense, what we discover in the Bible is the *family devalued*. To put it in biblical terms—and to invert Hillary Clinton's quintessential expression of family values—strong nations do not hinge upon strong families, at least not from a biblical perspective. Strong nations, rather, hinge upon the promise of God at work in the world despite—or even *through*—the dysfunction of families. Perfect families are not necessary for a great nation. A faithful God is.

Right from the start, in the first book of the Bible, the ancestor of Judaism, Christianity, and Islam blunders his way through family life. Abraham loses his nerve in Egypt and pawns his wife Sarah off as his sister because he is afraid that Pharaoh will murder him to get her (Gen. 12:10–20). Later, when he and Sarah find themselves old and childless, Sarah gives him her servant, Hagar, as a sexual partner (Gen. 16:1–16). Later still, Abraham takes another woman, Keturah, who bears him children (Gen. 25:1). A penchant for having children trumps family values.

Abraham even appears willing to take the knife to his son Isaac on Mount Moriah (Gen. 22:1–19). There is deep pathos in this story—but no defense of family values!

Isaac survives but remains, as on Mount Moriah, consistently passive. He does not search for a wife; instead, he sends a servant (Gen. 24:1–67). When he is blind and about to die, he blesses his sons, Jacob and Esau, while lying on his deathbed. Compare Isaac with his wife Rebecca, a whirlwind of activity when she meets Isaac's servant at a well. Rebecca tricks Isaac, on his deathbed, into giving Jacob, rather than Esau, a blessing (Gen. 27:1–28:5). Rebecca is the actor—we might call her the male lead—and Isaac the submissive partner in this marriage. And God works brilliantly through all of this to bring blessings to the nations.

Isaac and Rebecca's sons, Jacob and Esau, are hardly paradigms of virtue—especially Jacob, who compels his famished brother Esau to trade his birthright for a bowl of soup (Gen. 25:29–34).

And marriage? Jacob, tricked by his unlikeable uncle Laban, marries Leah, then her sister Rachel. Then, when Leah stops conceiving, Jacob has sex with Leah's servant Zilpah—hardly an action amenable to family values (Gen. 29:9–30:43).

On the contrary, Jacob has twelve sons by four women, sons who will carry God's promise to Egypt. The problem? Eleven of them conspire to be rid of their brother Joseph. This is more than dysfunction; it is abduction and attempted murder (Gen. 37:1–36). Still, God positions Joseph in Egypt, where he rises to power and rescues his family during a period of severe famine.

Faithless families. Faithful God. This is the message, through and through, of the first book of the Bible.

The second book, Exodus, begins with a villainous Pharaoh and unheralded heroes—not men but midwives, who refuse to follow Pharaoh's orders to slaughter baby boys (Exod. 1:1–22). Midwives had no children of their own and were, in family values' terms, valueless except to aid in birthing other women's children. Yet the second book of the Bible begins with them, before Moses ever happens upon the scene.

Israel's story continues with the undercurrent that feckless families cannot undercut God's faithfulness. King David, for example, whose story is marred by adultery with Bathsheba, murder of Bathsheba's husband Uriah (2 Sam. 11:1–12:25), incest and the rape of his daughter Tamar (2 Sam. 13:1–22), and an attempted coup by his son Absalom (2 Sam. 15:1–19:43), is hardly a paradigm of breadwinning virtue. The story of David is a family debacle. Yet God's promises are not thwarted by a lack of family values.

Finally, women, beyond the midwives, have books bearing their names because they are heroic in biblical terms. Ruth, still unmarried, snuggles up to a drunken Boaz and ends up as King David's great grandmother (Ruth 3:1–13). Esther, an Israelite woman in the Persian harem, saves her people (Esther 4:1–8:14). Judith, a widow, valiantly enters the tent of the enemy general, Holofernes, and cuts off his head (Judith 10:1–14:8).

Family values? Midwives: courageous, childless women. Ruth: a single woman risking a singularly risqué activity. Esther, the sexual property of an empire, rescuing a nation. And Judith, a widow, beheading the enemy. None of these women fits neatly into the honor role of family values, but all of them are pivotal to the enduring promise of God.

Families displaced

If what Christians call the Old Testament fails to offer a clinic in family values, surely the New Testament does? Not by a long shot.

Jesus, unmarried and itinerant, demands of his disciples a disregard for family. When Peter complains about leaving everything behind, Jesus replaces the family with a worldwide family of faith: "... [T]here is no one who has left house or brothers or sisters or mother or father or children or fields, for my sake and for the sake of the good news, who will not receive a hundredfold now in this age—houses, brothers and sisters, mothers and children, and fields, with persecutions—and in the age to come eternal life" (Mark 10:28–30; 3:31–35). Wherever his followers go for the sake of the good news, promises Jesus, they will discover a hospitable family of faith.

Where they will go is signaled by two words: *and persecution.* Jesus drives a wedge between loyalty to family and loyalty to himself when he predicts, "Brother will betray brother to death, and a father his child, and children will rise against parents and have them put to death; and you will be hated by all because of my name. But the one who endures to the end will be saved" (Mark 13:12–13).

In the Gospel of Luke, Jesus's demands are harsher still: "Whoever comes to me and does not hate father and mother, wife and children, brothers and sisters, yes, and even life itself, cannot be my disciple. Whoever does not carry the cross and follow me cannot be my disciple" (Luke 14:26–27). The version in Matthew's gospel is gentler: "Whoever loves father or mother more than me is not worthy of me; and whoever loves son or daughter more than me is not worthy of me; and whoever does not take up the cross and follow me is not worthy of me" (Matt. 10:37–38). Gentler, yes, but still a stiff rejection of family values.

We could say much to blunt the hard edge of Jesus's sayings. For instance, that they apply only to followers in Jesus's day: following Jesus led to persecution. Or that these are end of time sayings, which assume an imminent end, with persecutions. However, we blunt this edge, the conclusion is inevitable: *Jesus was no champion of family values.*

Leaders in the early church followed Jesus with an apparent disregard for family. They were typically either unmarried or inattentive to their spouses. The apostle Peter had a mother-in-law, but we hear nothing of his wife (Mark 1:30–31). The apostle Paul, in light of his clear preference for celibacy, may have been unmarried himself (1 Cor. 7:1–40).

In fact, the biblical basis for family values lies principally in the slender thread of a few short sections of a few New Testament letters, which advise women (or wives) to submit to men (or husbands), children to obey parents—and slaves to obey masters (e.g., Col. 3:18–4:1; Eph. 5:21–6:9; 1 Pet. 3:1–7). These are few and far between—and certainly not unambiguous safeguards of family values. For example, the command for women to submit to men in Ephesians 5:22 is preceded by the injunction, "Be subject to one another out of reverence for Christ." Submission of wife to husband is built upon the foundation of mutual submission.

The first family

When the dust settles, the founding story of family values occurs at the beginning. Skip, of course, the story of the first siblings, in which Cain murders his brother Abel. No model of family values there!

Turn instead to the creation of man and woman and their ousting from Eden—where family values find their point of origin. The woman is man's helpmeet, hardly his equal, proponents of family values contend. His authority is evident, further, in Adam's naming the woman, as he did the animals. And when they are cursed, the man is cursed in work, the woman in childbearing. This, from the standpoint of family values, is the proper order of creation, in which biological difference requires social difference: the man exercises authority, the woman submission.

Is this the true order of creation that was torn asunder by social upheavals in the 1970s? Not at all, and for more reasons than one.

First, when man sees woman, freshly created from his side, he notices *similarity* rather than difference. She is "*ishshah* [woman]," he says, "because she is made from *ish* [man]!" The first pun—wo*man* and *man*—cements the similarity between male and female *without* any recognition of difference (Gen. 2:23).

Second, the word "help," in Hebrew *ezer-kenegdo*, "helpmeet," is used almost exclusively of God's help throughout the Jewish scriptures (Gen. 2:18; see, e.g., Exod. 18:4; Deut. 33:7; Ps. 20:3; 70:6; 121:1). "Help" communicates salvation rather than service. The stronger helps the weaker; the liberator rescues the embattled. In Genesis 2, then, woman is created not for submission but for salvation; she is man's liberator, his savior. She is *like* the man. She corresponds to him. She alone, then, can rescue him from isolation.

Third, the man leaves his home (Gen. 2:24). The woman does not. This inverts the usual order of life, in which the woman joins the man's home.

The hierarchical order of life, with woman turning to her man, who rules over her, occurs only in the curses—not before (Gen. 3:16). Only *after* the curses, in fact, will man give woman a name: Eve (Gen. 3:20). The curses are, then, what is. They are not what should be.

What *should* be—ideal family values—is clear only *prior to* the first sin and the curses that distort man and woman's ideal relationship. They are *ish* and *ishshah*—man and woman—two peas in a pod, naked and unashamed. Woman is man's *savior-through-similarity*, his *ezer-kenegdo*, so much so that he leaves his home to join hers. Those are the family values of Eden, which disintegrate in the differences that too soon come to mark and mar Adam and Eve, Cain and Abel—the first family.

Works Cited

Balmer, Randall. *Redeemer: The Life of Jimmy Carter*. New York: Basic Books, 2011.
Clinton, Hillary. "Hillary Clinton's Campaign Announcement." April 12, 2015. http://www.nytimes.com/video/us/politics/100000003624500/hillary-clintons-announcement-video.html (accessed January 25, 2016).
"Democratic Party Platform of 1980." New York City, NY. August 11, 1980. http://www.presidency.ucsb.edu/ws/?pid=29607 (accessed January 26, 2016).
Dochuk, Darren. *From Bible Belt to Sun Belt: Plain-Folk Religion, Grassroots Politics, and the Rise of Evangelical Conservatism*. New York: W.W. Norton & Co., 2011.
Dowland, Seth. *Family Values and the Rise of the Christian Right*. Philadelphia: University of Pennsylvania Press, 2015.

Heltzel, Peter Goodwin. *Jesus and Justice*. New Haven: Yale University Press, 2009.

Kerry, John. "John Kerry's Acceptance Speech at Democratic National Convention." Boston, MA. July 29, 2004. http://www.washingtonpost .com/wp-dyn/articles/A25678-2004Jul29.html (accessed January 4, 2016).

Reagan, Ronald. "National Affairs Campaign Address." Dallas, TX. August 22, 1980. http://www.americanrhetoric.com/speeches/ ronaldreaganreligiousliberty.htm (accessed February 11, 2016).

"Republican Party Platform of 1980." Detroit, MI. July 15, 1980. http:// www.presidency.ucsb.edu/ws/?pid=25844 (accessed March 7, 2016).

Wetzstein, Cheryl. "Family-Values Groups Object to Obama's Orders on Immigration." *The Washington Times*. November 23, 2014. http:// www.washingtontimes.com/news/2014/nov/23/family-values-groups -object-to-obamas-orders-on-im/?page=all (accessed March 14, 2016).

Williams, Daniel K. *God's Own Party: The Making of the Christian Right*. New York: Oxford University Press, 2011.

2

Diasporas "R" Us: Attitudes toward Immigrants in the Bible

Hector Avalos

Judging by the rhetoric of the 2016 presidential candidates, one might surmise that American voters rank immigration as one of the most important issues in their lives. Indeed, on a nearly daily basis the media features the most inflammatory statements about immigrants by some candidates, mostly notably by Donald Trump.

Yet, polls show that immigration is not the top issue, or anything near the top issue, for most American voters. The Gallup organization, which has tracked the ranked importance of issues for voters since at least the 1950s, finds that only 8 percent of American voters named "immigration/illegal aliens" as the most important issue in their January 2016 poll.

Immigration does have a prominent presence in our political discourse. Immigration, especially in an era of globalization, can certainly change cultures and economies (Collier 2013). Conflict often results from migrations because competition for resources can ensue when people move into areas where others already have some claim to ownership or "citizenship."

Since the start of the Civil War in Syria in 2011, more than one million refugees have left that country. Large refugee camps in

Jordan, Turkey, and elsewhere struggle to provide the minimum in humanitarian aid. Many European countries that at first welcomed refugees from Syria and elsewhere are having second thoughts as nativists increasingly protest the arrival of foreigners. Fear of destabilizing the economy and cultures of Europe is cited as a reason for any hesitancy in aiding these refugees. The United Nations High Commissioner on Refugees estimates that globally 42,500 new refugees are created each day. In the case of the United States, the legal status of 11–12 million undocumented immigrants is a key discussion item in the 2016 presidential election debates.

Such national and global developments surrounding immigration have prompted many people who use the Bible as an authority to ask themselves: To what extent should followers of biblical principles help or give sanctuary to immigrants, and especially to those who are undocumented? What does the Bible really say?

Since legal immigration is not what dominates most of our political discourse, I will concentrate on how the Bible has been used in sociopolitical debates about undocumented (or "illegal") immigrants living in the United States. As mentioned, the fate of the 11–12 million undocumented persons living in the United States is at stake.

Presidential candidates in the 2016 presidential race fall along a spectrum of immigration policies that can range from encouraging acceptance and facilitating legalization of undocumented immigrants to opposing and even deporting all undocumented immigrants. The most extreme anti-immigrant position is perhaps that of Donald Trump, the presumptive Republican nominee at the time of this writing. Trump has called for the deportation of all undocumented immigrants in this country, even if that means separating undocumented parents from children who are citizens by virtue of being born in the United States. Trump has also called for at least a temporary ban on all Muslims entering the United States, even if they are otherwise American citizens or legally eligible for immigration (On the Issues 2016).

President Barack Obama has deported as many or more individuals, mainly those with criminal records, than his predecessor, George W. Bush (Terrio 2015, 16). Nonetheless, Obama has spoken out against mass deportations and signed executive orders, now in federal litigation, that would allow about five million people, and especially those brought to the United States as children, through the Deferred Action on Childhood Arrivals program, to remain in the United States. President Obama paraphrases scripture (e.g., Lev. 19:33–34) to undergird his stance: "Scripture tells us that we shall not oppress a stranger, for we know the heart of a stranger—we were strangers once, too. My fellow Americans, we are and always will be a nation of immigrants. We were strangers once, too" (Obama 2014).

What does the Bible really say?

At least two positions can be identified among those who appeal to the Bible to formulate their responses to undocumented immigrants:

1   A legocentric position (law-centered), which describes those who believe any aid to immigrants must be undertaken in conformity with national laws even if it means expelling undocumented persons en masse. Although other names have been applied to this position, I follow scholars of comparative law in adapting the more formal term "legocentric" to describe this view (Reimann and Zimmerman 2008, 691).

2   A non-legocentric position, which describes those who believe that national laws do not take precedence over humanitarian and "higher" laws.

3   By contrast, a position that I call "post-scripturalism" argues that sacred texts are not useful in formulating any modern policies regarding immigration, and sacred texts should not be used as moral authorities in any case.

The rest of this chapter will explore how the legocentric, non-legocentric, and post-scriptualist positions view the role of the Bible. As a biblical scholar who happens to be an atheist, I do not use the Bible to favor either the legocentric or non-legocentric position. Rather, my task is to understand what the biblical texts are saying in their original contexts. I also see my task as challenging religiocentric and bibliocentric biases that often permeate all arguments that do appeal to the Bible as an authority.

In order to understand the discussion among these positions, one first must understand what I mean by "the Bible." As the later chapter in this volume by Kelley Coblentz Bautch explains, the definition of "Bible" differs over time and depends on the religious context. In general, I am restricting myself to the Protestant and Catholic canons of the Bible, which have sixty-six and seventy-two (or seventy-three) books, respectively. The main reason is that this is what my expected readership regards as "the Bible."

Second, the Bible was written over a span of centuries by authors with different ideological and religious agendas. Some of their ideas about immigration, ethnic identity, and nationalism are very different from our own, and so one must be cautious when making cultural comparisons.

Third, we should not expect biblical authors to agree with themselves on every issue any more than we should expect modern Jews and Christians to agree on every issue. In general, the more conservative approaches to the Bible emphasize unity and seek to harmonize all of the biblical authors. On the other hand, the more "liberal" and historical-critical approaches see much diversity, tension, and contradiction in biblical positions.

Finally, much of the debate centers on the meaning of particular words used in Hebrew and Greek. For example, the Hebrew word that is one of the most frequently discussed is *gēr*. Depending on the biblical version or scholar, it has been translated as "sojourner," "immigrant," "stranger," or "resident alien," among others. There are questions about the historical evolution in the use of these terms, and also in how different literary traditions within the Bible use them (Van Houten 1991).

Yet, none of these translations of *gēr* or *tôshab*, another related term, may be quite the equivalent of our "undocumented" or "illegal" alien. There were not any "documents" that people carried around in ancient Israel describing their citizenship status. A *gēr* may be someone from another tribe, and not just from another nation. All of these linguistic issues complicate any search for what the Bible "really says" about undocumented immigration.

The non-legocentric position in biblical studies

Many studies of immigration in biblical scholarship support the view of non-legocentrism (e.g., Carroll 2008; Houston 2015; Myers and Colwell 2012; Smith-Christopher 2007). The non-legocentric position argues that secular law should not be the main determinant in how to address the issues of undocumented immigration. There are degrees to which the law should be followed, but this position holds that humanitarian grounds are primary. Furthermore, it holds that the Bible supports this position.

On a broader theological level, this position emphasizes that all human beings are created in the image of God. For M. Daniel Carroll R, "the creation of all persons in the image of God must be the most basic conviction for Christians as they approach the challenges of immigration today" (Carroll 2008, 67). Rights that human beings have by virtue of being made in the image of God must take precedence over national borders or economics.

Among the most prominent passages used by non-legocentrists is Leviticus 19:33–34: "When an alien resides with you in your land, you shall not oppress the alien. The alien who resides with you shall be to you as the citizen among you; you shall love the alien as yourself, for you were aliens in the land of Egypt. I am the LORD your God" (see also Exod. 23:9; Deut. 10:18–19; and Heb. 13:1).

Ched Myers and Matthew Colwell, who have been very active in The Sanctuary Movement, emphasize that "the principle of sanctuary was codified in Torah through the establishment of 'cities of refuge'" in Exod. 21:13 and Num. 35:9–28 (Myers and Colwell 2012, 56). For Myers and Colwell, such a principle authorizes Christians to defy national laws to protect and give sanctuary, whether in churches or in cities, to undocumented individuals.

The non-legocentric position sometimes notes that Jesus himself was a refugee (Carroll 2008, 115–116; Houston 2015, 134–136). According to the Office of the United Nations High Commissioner for Refugees, refugees are "persons fleeing armed conflict or persecution. ..." (UNHCR 2015).

The UNHCR distinguishes refugees from migrants—persons who "choose to move not because of a direct threat of persecution or death, but mainly to improve their lives by finding work, or in some cases for education, family reunion, or other reasons" (UNHCR 2015). It is assumed that migrants can safely return home. Jesus in the Gospel of Matthew (2:1–15) would qualify as a refugee because his life was endangered by the policies of Herod the Great.

Popular among non-legocentrists is the story of the Good Samaritan (Luke 10:25–37), who helped a wounded man without first asking about his ethnic, religious, or legal status. Jesus's concluding instruction is: "Go and do likewise" (Carroll 2008, 121).

Finding analogies between ancient biblical narratives and modern immigrant populations is an important part of making the case for mercy toward immigrants (Ruiz 2011, 18). Examples include Gregory Cuellar's *Second Isaiah 40–55 and the Mexican Immigrant Experience* (2008) and Virgilio Elizondo's *Galilean Journey: The Mexican-American Promise* (1983).

Also popular are Jesus's statements in Matthew 25:40, 42–43 (RSV): "And the King will answer them, 'Truly, I say to you, as you did it to one of the least of these my brethren, you did it to me … for I was hungry and you gave me no food, I was thirsty and you gave me no drink, I was a stranger and you did not welcome me, naked and you did not clothe me, sick and in prison and you did not visit me.'"

However, not all non-legocentric scholars believe that "my brethren" refers to everyone. For Carroll, "the least of these my brethren" refers only to fellow Christians, and not all human beings (Carroll 2008, 123). Houston and other non-legocentric scholars interpret this passage to mean that Christians have an obligation to care for all disadvantaged human beings, including immigrants in need (Houston 2015, 145).

When laws conflict with humanitarian values, then the solution is offered by Acts 4:19 (see also Acts 5:29), where Peter and John challenge secular law with this response: "Whether it is right in God's sight to listen to you rather than to God, you must judge." Carroll (2008, 132) quotes this passage to argue that it must take precedence over Romans 13:1–7, which is often quoted by those who believe God demands that Christians follow all earthly laws.

In general, higher divine and humanitarian needs supersede secular laws. Accordingly, undocumented immigrants, and especially refugees fleeing violence, deserve to be helped even if it sometimes contravenes national laws.

The legocentric position
in biblical studies

James K. Hoffmeier, who is the main representative of this position, describes as the "law-and-order camp" those who are for bestowing primacy on the law of the land when addressing the issue of undocumented immigrants (Hoffmeier 2009, 22; see also Tooley 2014).

Although Hoffmeier (2009, 17) indicates that he did not intend his book to be a response to Carroll, the fact is that he does respond directly to some of Carroll's main arguments. After surveying many of the biblical passages dealing with immigration, Hoffmeier (2009, 146) concludes: "I see nothing in Scripture that would abrogate current immigration laws."

As mentioned, the meaning and usage of key words are where the debates often center. Hoffmeier (2009, 52) argues that the Hebrew word gēr usually translated as "sojourner," "alien," or "stranger" refers to authorized or legal residents who respected the borders of their host countries.

Hoffmeier adds that borders did exist, and Israel often had to ask for permission to cross them, as in Judges 11:17: "Israel then sent messengers to the king of Edom, saying, 'Let us pass through your land'; but the king of Edom would not listen. They also sent to the king of Moab, but he would not consent. So Israel remained at Kadesh." Jacob sought permission from Pharaoh in Genesis 47:4: "We have come to reside as aliens in the land; for there is pasture for your servants' flocks because the famine is severe in the land of Canaan. Now we ask you, let your servants settle in the land of Goshen."

Romans 13:1–7 is a key text for Hoffmeier, who remarks "governments are ordained by God, and laws and ordinances made by human, unless they clearly violate divine principles or teaching, should be followed" (Hoffmeier 2009, 152). Exceptions might include violating a law in order to save a human life, as in the case of the Hebrew midwives in Exodus 1:15–21. In that case, God rewarded the midwives for not following Pharaoh's laws. According to Hoffmeier, such disobedience to national laws today might biblically allow a health-care professional to refuse to perform abortions in a hospital.

More importantly for the immigration debate, Hoffmeier (2009, 147) argues that "breaking immigration laws to improve one's economic standard does not rise to the same moral level as a medical professional refusing to perform an abortion." Similarly, Hoffmeier (2009, 81) argues that "sanctuaries" in the Hebrew Bible were meant to protect those who had accidentally killed someone, and not those who violate borders.

Overall, Hoffmeier (2009, 145) argues that "for Carroll's position to have merit, current American laws must be inherently unjust." Aiding the undocumented might include being an intermediate between the government and the undocumented individual in the effort to find legal solutions to any current plight. Anything beyond that is not "biblical" for Hoffmeier.

The post-scripturalist position

The post-scripturalist position affirms that sacred scriptures are neither useful nor morally authoritative in solving any social problems today, including immigration. Aside from objections to the use of theology in any area of biblical studies, the main post-scripturalist objections to both the legocentric and non-legocentric views may be outlined as follows:

1   The Bible offers both pro-immigrant and anti-immigrant sentiments, and so it is arbitrary to choose one or the other as representative of the Bible's "core" or "essential" message.

2   The texts chosen to represent each stance usually overlook other problems or are permeated by a bibliolatrous perspective, which deems the Bible as offering a superior set of ethics when compared to nonbiblical cultures.

3   Advocates of both sides often omit or do not fully address texts that are not consistent with their respective positions.

In regard to the first point, even some non-legocentric scholars grant that both pro-immigrant and anti-immigrant sentiments can be found in the Bible. As Daniel L. Christopher-Smith notes, "... [B]igoted attitudes toward foreigners (especially the threat of foreign women) complete with pejorative terms, also co-existed within Israelite society with more open and welcoming attitudes" (Smith-Christopher 1996, 129–130).

For example, the prohibition in Deuteronomy 23:3 ("No Ammonite or Moabite shall be admitted to the assembly of the LORD. Even to the tenth generation, none of their descendants shall be admitted to assembly of the LORD") shows that not all immigrants are to be treated equally. The basis for discrimination can be religious, cultural, or some past transgression for which the descendants are held responsible.

On the other hand, both the legocentric and non-legocentric rightly show that there are passages (Exod. 23:9 and Lev. 19:33–34) instructing Israelites to treat migrants and strangers well. The problem is determining what "treating immigrants and strangers well" really means.

After all, the same book of Leviticus prohibits Hebrews from owning fellow Hebrews, but yet allows them to own non-Hebrews (Lev. 25:44–46). Making distinctions between Hebrews and non-Hebrews insofar as slavery is concerned does not reflect an ideology where strangers are to be treated the same as natives.

Jesus lauds the man who helps the Samaritan without regard to ethnicity or national origin. On the other hand, Jesus uses a denigrating epithet for foreigners ("dogs") and seems hesitant to help the Syro-Phoenician woman in Matthew 15:21–28 (Mark 7:24–30) until she declares his lordship (Avalos 2015, 235–244).

Hoffmeier can point to Romans 13 to claim that God has set up laws and Christians must obey them. However, Carroll can argue that Acts 4:19 (and Acts 5:29) allows Christians to violate laws when they conflict with God's laws. The dispute about what counts as a valid exception ultimately devolves into a theological argument that cannot be adjudicated by any objective means.

Both the legocentric and non-legocentric positions overlook problems in the texts chosen to represent them. Consider Leviticus 24:22, a text cited by both the legocentric and non-legocentric position: "You shall have one law for the alien and for the citizen: for I am the LORD your God."

Although the idea of having one law for the native and for the foreigner appears to be friendly to immigrants, it can mean that immigrants will be subject to various penalties for religious practices that do not conform to the host's religion. In the case of ancient Israel, it may mean that immigrants can also be put to death for not observing the Sabbath laws (Exod. 31:15). This sort of "equal" treatment would not be dissimilar from that of any other modern culture or political entity that allows only one religion, and punishes both natives and immigrants who do not conform to that accepted religion.

Ruth is one of the most famous exemplars of an immigrant-friendly attitude cited by both the legocentric and non-legocentric camps (Hoffmeier 2009, 103–107; Carroll 2008, 74–75). Nevertheless, Laura Donaldson has pointed out that Ruth was accepted only because she was willing to give up her religion and culture. In other words, Ruth is an example of how acceptance by Hebrew culture demanded her Moabite deculturation (Donaldson 1999). A similar observation holds for Isaiah 56:1–7, where foreigners seem well accepted as long as they submit to the religion of Israel.

Likewise, legocentrists and non-legocentrists both use the Exodus as a paradigm of liberation for oppressed Israelites. In this case, both views often overlook the fact that the ultimate goal of reaching the Promised Land would involve the genocide and enslavement of Canaanites whose land the Israelites would take. So, Exodus can also be read as a case where any liberation is for the benefit of the Hebrews, and not for every other oppressed group of immigrants or refugees.

The directive to "love your neighbor as yourself" in Leviticus 19:18 is not as clear as some may think. Some scholars argue that "neighbors" refers only to fellow Israelites, while others interpret it more expansively. If by citing this verse Jesus changed a more original meaning that was more restrictive, then his authority to change the meaning rests on a theological presupposition that he has such authority to reinterpret scripture (Avalos 2015, 32–33, 376).

The concept of being made in the image of God is often assumed to mean that all human beings are accorded equal human rights by both legocentrists and non-legocentrists. However, being made in the image of God afforded no protection to the Canaanites who were destroyed because they had a different religion and culture.

Fear of embedded terrorists among the refugees is one of the most significant reasons for rejecting the acceptance of Syrians into western countries. That fear is cited by Donald Trump and

Ted Cruz as a reason against any open acceptance of these refugees into the United States. Yet, this attitude also has potential biblical precedents.

The Canaanites, who themselves became internal refugees after the Hebrew conquest, were to be slaughtered because they were potential threats to the religion of God's chosen people in Deuteronomy 20:16–18: "But as for the towns of these peoples that the LORD your God is giving you as an inheritance, you must not let anything that breathes remain alive. You shall annihilate them...that they may not teach you to do all the abhorrent things that they do in the service for their gods, and you thus sin against the LORD your God." Hoffmeier (2009, 165) does not include this text in his scriptural index.

Neither Hoffmeier nor Carroll adequately address Ezra 9–10, where Ezra, the priest and leader of the repatriated exiles, demands that Jewish husbands send away their foreign wives and their children of those marriages. Ezra's instructions intend to rid Israel of foreign influences: "[L]et us make a covenant with our God to send away all these wives and their children, according to the counsel of my lord and of those who tremble at the commandment of our God; and let it be done according to the law" (Ezra 10:3).

Ezra's attitude toward people of different religion could support those who argue that the Bible allows the deportation of people on the basis of their religion, even if it means separating fathers from their children. Ezra's position would provide support for those who argue that difference in culture or religion can be a justifiable reason for deportation.

Even if post-scripturalists hold that the Bible may not be useful in setting social policy on immigration, they would not deny that it does have some historically important lessons. Perhaps the most important lesson is that biblical texts show how there have been three recurrent methods to deal with unwanted populations from ancient to modern times: (1) genocide, (2) enslavement, and (3) exile. These are all illustrated in Exodus 1–12, when the Egyptian Pharaoh views the multiplication of the Hebrews as a problem.

At any one time today, governments are still using one or more of these policies to deal with unwanted populations. Nazi Germany, of course, is infamous for using genocide against Jews and other unwanted populations. In Syria, genocide and exile are being used by the Bashar Hafez al-Assad regime against those who oppose him. In the United States, some politicians openly advocate for mass deportation, mainly for Latino immigrants. Virtual enslavement exists in many western countries for many immigrants—both legal and illegal—who find they must work as domestic housekeepers, sex workers, or in the agricultural sector.

For the secular post-scripturalists, a biblical view on immigration is irrelevant because it is immoral to use a sacred text to authorize any moral behavior or social policy. Furthermore, post-scripturalists affirm that we should love our neighbors not because a text or deity tells us to do so, but because we have the ability to empathize with other human beings.

Conclusion

We are all the consequence of a diaspora at some point in the past. Indeed, migration is a constant feature of our planet. Almost all organisms move from their original place of birth, whether these organisms are our smallest viruses or our largest animal species. Human beings were born in Africa, but we have now stepped on all parts of the globe, and even on the moon.

Conflicts often ensue when organisms, human or nonhuman, compete for the same resources and territories. The Bible certainly shows that conflicts about borders and migration are nothing new. Addressing the consequences of diasporas and migrations is now seen by some scholars as essential features of Judaism and early Christianity (Charles 2014). Regardless of whether or not the Bible is regarded as a useful theological or ethical manual for today, educated citizens must understand the views of those who use the Bible to guide their social policies on immigration.

Ultimately, any increased acceptance of immigrants, documented or not, will need to find a balance between our human empathy and the capacity of our economic resources to assist those immigrants. On a more politically realistic level, any efforts to integrate documented and undocumented immigrants must center on convincing the "natives" of any country that the benefits outweigh any loss of security and well-being for their society.

Works Cited

Avalos, Hector. *The Bad Jesus: The Ethics of New Testament Ethics*. Sheffield: Sheffield Phoenix Press, 2015.

Carroll, R.M. Daniel. *Christians at the Border: Immigration, the Church, and the Bible*. Grand Rapids, MI: Baker Academic, 2008.

Charles, Ronald. *Paul and the Politics of Diaspora*. Minneapolis, MN: Fortress Press, 2014.

Collier, Paul. *Exodus: How Migration Is Changing Our World*. New York: Oxford University Press, 2013.

Cruz, Ted. 2016. https://www.tedcruz.org/issues/secure-the-border/ (accessed March 25, 2016).

Cuellar, Gregory Lee. *Voices of Marginality: Exile and Return in Second Isaiah 40–55 and the Mexican Immigrant Experience*. New York: Peter Lang, 2008.

Donaldson, Laura E. "The Sign of Orpah: Reading Ruth through Native Eyes." In *Ruth and Esther: A Feminist Companion to the Bible*, edited by Athalya Brenner, 130–144. Second Series. Sheffield: Sheffield Academic Press, 1999.

Elizondo, Virgilio. *Galilean Journey: The Mexican American Promise*. Maryknoll, NY: Orbis Books, 1983.

Gallup Organization Polls. "Most Important Problem." http://www.gallup.com/poll/1675/most-important-problem.aspx (accessed February 1, 2016).

Hoffmeier, James K. *The Immigration Crisis: Immigrants, Aliens, and the Bible* Wheaton, IL: Crossway Books, 2009.

Houston, Fleur S. *You Shall Love the Stranger as Yourself: The Bible, Refugees, and Asylum*. New York: Routledge, 2015.

Marco, Rubio. 2016. "How Marco Will Start Securing Our Border on Day One." https://marcorubio.com/issues-2/marco-rubio-immigration-plan-border-security-legal/ (accessed March 2, 2016).

Myers, Ched and Colwell, Matthew. *Our God Is Undocumented: Biblical Faith and Immigrant Justice*. Maryknoll, NY: Orbis Books, 2012.

Obama, Barack. The White House, Office of the Press Secretary. "Remarks by the President in Address to the Nation on Immigration." November 20, 2014. https://www.whitehouse.gov/the-press-office/2014/11/20/remarks-president-address-nation-immigration (accessed March 10, 2016).

On the Issues. Donald Trump. http://www.ontheissues.org/Donald_Trump.htm#Immigration (accessed March 1, 2016).

Reimann, Mathias and Zimmerman, Reinhard (eds.). *The Oxford Handbook of Comparative Law*. New York: Oxford University Press, 2008.

Ruiz, Jean-Pierre, *Readings from the Edges: The Bible and People on the Move*. Maryknoll, NY: Orbis Books, 2011.

Smith-Christopher, Daniel L. "Between Ezra and Nehemiah: Exclusion, Transformation, and Inclusion of the Foreigner in Post-Exilic Biblical Theology." In *Ethnicity and the Bible*, edited by Mark G. Brett, 117–142. Leiden: E. J. Brill, 1996.

Smith-Christopher, Daniel L. *Jonah, Jesus, and Other Good Coyotes: Speaking Peace to Power in the Bible*. Nashville: Abingdon, 2007.

Terrio, Susan J. *Whose Child Am I? Unaccompanied, Undocumented Children in U.S. Immigration Custody*. Berkeley: University of California Press, 2015.

Tooley, Mark. "Christian Response to Executive Amnesty?" November 19, 2014. Institute on Religion and Democracy. http://www.theird.org/ (accessed February 10, 2016).

UNHCR. "'Refugee' or 'Migrant'—Which Is Right?" August 27, 2015. http://www.unhcr.org/55df0e556.html (accessed March 5, 2016).

Van Houten, Christiana. *The Alien in Israelite Law*. Sheffield: JSOT Press, 1991.

3

Ending a Life That Has Not Begun—Abortion in the Bible

Bert Jan Lietaert Peerbolte

The topic of abortion, the ending of a pregnancy by the externally induced removal of the fetus, strongly divides American public opinion. Roughly speaking, the two extreme positions are those of the pro-life movement ("life is sacred and abortion is murder") and the pro-choice movement ("a woman has the right to decide whether or not to continue her pregnancy"). Although the famous *Roe v. Wade* case of 1973 settled the law in favor of a woman's right to choose, that case still forms the eye of a storm. Not only do politicians sometimes promise to overturn *Roe v. Wade*, other legal challenges with alternative arguments have mounted. For instance, some proposed laws have raised the issue of when a fetus may legally be considered a person, with the full rights of a U.S. citizen. The U.S. Supreme Court is currently weighing the constitutionality of Texas laws implemented in 2013 that place rigorous new regulations on abortion clinics, with the effect that half had already closed by 2016 (Goodnough 2016).

In their attempts to gain the support of evangelical and other conservative Christian voters, Republican candidates have stumbled over each other in order to point out that their political views are founded on traditional Christian views and values. Donald Trump, the Republican frontrunner for the Presidency at the time of this writing, held a pro-choice stance until very recently. In 2016, he has announced that he is pro-life, with limited exceptions for terminating a pregnancy. In this and other policy decisions, Trump seems to be appealing to an evangelical Christian voter base. He has called the Bible his favorite book, saying "The Book, it is the thing." However, his knowledge of the Bible seems to be shallow. In an address at the evangelical Liberty University in Virginia, he referred to 2 Corinthians 3:17 incorrectly by saying "Two Corinthians 3:17, that's the whole ballgame!" At an earlier occasion, Trump had answered the question as to which verse in the Bible would be his favorite by referring to a chapter (!) in Proverbs no other reader of the Bible has been able to find: "Proverbs, chapter 'never bend to envy.'"

Other Republican candidates claim the Bible legitimates their views on abortion (and other issues) as well. Senator Marco Rubio referred to his biblical faith as the foundation of his views on the sacred character of life, although Senator Ted Cruz questioned Rubio's faith in response. Cruz holds a more extreme position. He has given numerous interviews and speeches in which he has actually favored a theocratic ideal: it is God who should rule the United States. Some of the major promises of Cruz's campaign have been to defund Planned Parenthood and battle abortion.

All political rhetoric aside, it is important to note that various politicians and pundits assume that the Bible clearly speaks out against abortion and claim that this biblical view should be granted authority today. Let us, for that reason, focus on two specific questions. First, how does the Bible actually speak about abortion? Second, how should the authority of the Bible be valued in a complex discussion like the one on abortion?

Abortion and infanticide in early Judaism and early Christianity

In an evident display of anti-Judaism, the Roman historian Tacitus (ca. 56–120 C.E.) gives a survey of a variety of Jewish characteristics he considers "base and abominable" (*Histories* 5,5).

Among various characteristics, Tacitus describes how Jews set themselves apart from other human beings by abstaining from table fellowship with non-Jews, and how they deny the traditional gods their existence. The list of accusations Tacitus brings against Jewish customs is interesting from a cultural point of view: Tacitus basically reproaches the Jews for not being Romans and for practicing all kinds of habits that go against the grain of Roman culture. One of the more telling complaints Tacitus describes is this: "… [T]hey take thought to increase their numbers; for they regard it as a crime to kill any late-born child, and they believe that the souls of those who are killed in battle or by the executioner are immortal: hence comes their passion for begetting children, and their scorn of death" (Stern 1980, 26).

Tacitus's reference to the Jewish disapproval of killing late-born children indicates how the cultural clash between Jews and Romans became manifest at this specific point. It was a widely practiced Roman custom to actively or passively kill unwanted children shortly after they were born (Stern 1980, 41). The philosopher Seneca, for instance, describes how parents would expose defective children and refers to this as a completely natural thing: "Mad dogs we knock on the head; the fierce and savage ox we slay; sickly sheep we put to the knife to keep them from infecting the flock; unnatural progeny we destroy; we drown even children who at birth are weakly and abnormal." This habit is also attested for healthy children who were unwelcome for economic or other reasons.

Emerging Christianity followed in the footsteps of its Jewish pre-history and took an explicit stand against these practices. The second-century Christian author Tertullian wrote a defense of Christianity and criticized the habits of infanticide and abortion. Tertullian first explains how the killing of children is wrong: "[T]here is no difference as to baby-killing whether you do it as a sacred rite or just because you choose to do it" (*Apology* 9,6). Tertullian adds, by the way, that the killing of one's own child is not the same as murder. The background to this remark is the Roman legal principle that children belong to the property of their father and, therefore, the father has the legal right to destroy his property (i.e., kill his own child). He mentions the various methods by which children are killed in the Roman world: "[T]o choke out the breath in water or to expose to cold, starvation and the dogs" (*Apology* 9,7). The general principle according to which Tertullian rejects infanticide as well as abortion is this: "For us murder is once for all forbidden; so even the child in the womb, while yet the mother's blood is still being drawn on to form the human being, it is not lawful for us to destroy. To forbid birth is only quicker murder. It makes no difference whether one take away the life once born or destroy it as it comes to birth. He is a man, who is to be a man; the fruit is always present in the seed" (*Apology* 9,8). Other apologists followed in Tertullian's wake. Thus, Christianity in its formative stage took over a Jewish line of reasoning that clearly set it apart from its surrounding pagan culture: abortion and infanticide are regarded as unlawful.

Tertullian's view has become the standard view of the orthodox Catholic tradition (Flannagan 2012, 59–60). Basically, the line of reasoning is quite simple: since every human being is a person given by God, life should be protected in all its forms. The killing of human beings should be seen as murder and, thus, the killing of a fetus falls under that verdict, too.

The sanctity of human life

The creation narratives of Genesis 1–2 depict God as the one who gives life to the first human beings. Genesis 1:26–27 indicates that God "created mankind in his own image" without any details on what exactly happened and how this came about. However, a verse from the second creation narrative (Gen. 2:7) explicitly states that the breath of life is given to man by God. By implication, this is considered the moment at which "man became a living being" (see Cassuto 1961, 106). It is this particular account that has functioned as the legitimation of the concept of the sanctity of human life throughout the history of interpretation of the Book of Genesis.

The preservation of human life is one of the most important commandments in the Ten Commandments, both in Exodus 20:13 and in Deuteronomy 5:17: "[Y]ou shall not murder." It is remarkable that Jesus quotes this particular commandment as the first in the series he mentions in Mark 10:19–20: "You know the commandments: 'You shall not murder, you shall not commit adultery, you shall not steal, you shall not give false testimony, you shall not defraud, honor your father and mother'" (see Matt. 19:18 and Luke 18:20; Gnilka 1979, 86–87).

It is clear that the Hebrew Bible considers life as a gift from God, and ancient Israel took a sharp stand against the sacrifice of children. Life is considered holy and should therefore be defended. The sacrifice of children is presented as the ultimate example of the ungodly behavior of the nations outside of Israel, which is sometimes copied by the Israelites who are then fiercely rebuked for this (cf. Deut. 12:31; 18:10; 2 Kgs. 16:3; 17:17; Ps. 106:37–38; Jer. 7:27–31; and Ezek. 16:20–21; 23:36–39).

The narrative of Genesis 22 clearly alludes to the practice of the ritual killing of children as must have been present among the nations that surrounded Israel. In this chapter, Abraham is told to go out with his only son to the region of Moriah. The instruction is simple: "Sacrifice him there as a burnt offering on a mountain I will show you." Isaac initially does not understand the nature of the sacrifice and, by the time he does, a divine intervention prevents Abraham from killing his son. One element in the message that this story may convey is that Israel's God does not want the sacrifice of children, but the dedication of the believer (Noort and Tigchelaar 2002). The brief but compelling mention of Ahaz's sacrifice of his own son in 1 Kings 16:3 evidently pictures the king as committing one of the worst crimes imaginable. It is thus clear that the religion of Israel distanced itself from existing religious practices in the ancient Near East and condemned the practice of the ritual killing of children.

The God-given character of human life is probably best illustrated in a series of texts that relate God to life instead of death. Thus, the Wisdom of Solomon, a book in the Catholic Apocrypha, states that God made life, but not death:

Do not invite death by the error of your life,
or bring on destruction by the works of your hands;
because God did not make death,
and he does not delight in the death of the living.
For he created all things so that they might exist;
the generative forces of the world are wholesome,
and there is no destructive poison in them,
and the dominion of Hades is not on earth.
For righteousness is immortal. (1:12–15)

This writing probably dates back to the first century B.C.E. and indicates that the author believes that God is the originator of life, not death. Human beings have the capacity to choose death over life, since righteousness equals the way of life. Evidence from the Hebrew Bible, supported by other ancient Jewish texts, indicates that life is thought to stem from God and is therefore considered as sacred. This idea is clearly taken up and continued in the New Testament.

Thus, approaching the question of abortion from the perspective of the sacred character of life can certainly be underpinned with biblical references (see also Verhey 2003). Now if we can safely say that the divine origin of life led to a high esteem for life in the biblical tradition, the debate on abortion raises a fundamental question: when does human life begin?

When does life begin?

It is here that the difficulties begin, since a number of biblical texts appear to reflect different ideas about this. In defending his authority as a leader to the church in Galatia, the apostle Paul argues: "God, who set me apart from my mother's womb and called me by his grace, was pleased to reveal his Son in me so that I might preach him among the Gentiles ..." (Gal. 1:15). The reference here may draw from the writings of a prophet, Jeremiah, who claimed a similar status. Jeremiah wrote that God said to him: "Before I formed you in the womb I knew you, before you were born I set you apart; I appointed you as a prophet to the nations" (Jer. 1:5). A similar thought occurs in the writings of a prophet in the Book of Isaiah: "Before I was born the Lord called me" (Isa. 49:1).

These verses are often referred to as proof of the fact that, according to the Bible, the human being is already a living person in the womb, for whom God may have special plans. This would in fact mean that human life should be seen as beginning at the conception of the fetus and not at the moment of birth.

In the Book of Numbers, a census is taken with the following instructions: "The Lord said to Moses, 'Count all the firstborn Israelite males who are a month old or more and make a list of their names'" (Num. 3:40). The situation can only be explained if we assume that life was considered to really begin after one month. This text seems to reflect a practice also found in the instructions for the registration of Levites, a class of Temple servants, which is found in the same book (Num. 3:15). There, too, it is stated that all male persons aged one month or more should be registered in the list of the Levites. It would appear that in this book, infants under the age of one month are not yet counted as full persons.

The same Book of Numbers contains a piece of legislation in 5:11–31, which is not at all easy to interpret (Verhey 2003, 201–203). This particular passage deals with the situation in which a wife has had sexual intercourse with a man other than her husband. The text states that if this is uncertain and her husband distrusts her, the same ritual is to be performed as when the adultery is proven. The wife shall approach the priest in the temple, who will utter a formula to her and subsequently will give her a magic potion to drink. What happens next depends on the biblical translation that one reads.

The English translation in the New International Version implies in Numbers 5:22 that the potion will induce a miscarriage, thereby suggesting that this passage speaks about a precept for abortion in case of adultery. In fact, what exactly happens to the woman's womb is unclear—the Hebrew verb used here means "to swell." Thus, it seems that Numbers 5:11–31 does not explicitly deal with abortion. However, the drinking of the potion does aim at having an abortive effect in case the woman has indeed had illicit sexual contact outside her marriage. The magical ritual works automatically, either the woman becomes infertile and is proven guilty or the woman is "cleared of guilt and will be able to have children" (Num. 5:28).

There is one passage in particular in the legal portion of the Hebrew Bible that deals with the injury of a pregnant woman that may shed light on ancient Israelite legal views of a fetus (Verhey 2003, 198–201). Exodus 21:22–25 states: "If people are fighting and hit a pregnant woman and she gives birth prematurely but there is no serious injury, the offender must be fined whatever the woman's husband demands and the court allows. But if there is serious injury, you are to take life for life, eye for eye, tooth for tooth, hand for hand, foot for foot, burn for burn, wound for wound, bruise for bruise." The difficulty in this passage is that it is unclear in the Hebrew text whether the "serious injury" concerns the mother or the fetus.

Early Greek translations of the Hebrew Bible clear up a number of ambiguities in the passage. These translations inserted a clarifying statement into the text: the situation changes once the fetus is "fully formed." An English translation of the Greek of the passage goes as follows: "Now if two men fight and strike a pregnant woman and her child comes forth not fully formed, he shall be punished with a fine. According as the husband of the woman might impose, he shall pay with judicial assessment. But if it is fully formed, he shall pay life for life, eye for eye, tooth for tooth, hand for hand, foot for foot, burn for burn, wound for wound, stripe for stripe" (Perkins 2009).

The first-century Jewish philosopher Philo of Alexandria discusses this same passage in one of his works. There, Philo gives his own version of the passage, probably going back to a Greek version of it, and summarizes the commandment as follows:

> If a man comes to blows with a pregnant woman and strikes her on the belly and she miscarries, then, if the result of the miscarriage is unshaped and undeveloped, he must be fined both for the outrage and for obstructing the artist Nature in her creative work of bringing into life the fairest of living creatures, man. But, if the offspring is already shaped and all the limbs have their proper qualities and places in the system, he must die, for that which answers to this description is a human being, which he has destroyed in the laboratory of Nature who judges that the hour has not yet come for bringing it out into the light, like a statue lying in a studio requiring nothing more than to be conveyed outside and released from confinement. (Philo, *Special Laws* III,108–109)

Philo applies this argument to infanticide, a practice well known in his day, which is the actual practice he intends to attack. According to Philo, the exposure of children is a punishable sin. This is absolutely clear from the instruction of Exodus 21:22–25: "For if on behalf of the child not yet brought to the birth by the appointed conclusion of the regular period thought has to be taken to save it from disaster at the hands of the evil-minded, surely still more true is this of the full-born babe...." (Philo, *Special Laws* III,111).

Modern legislation both in the United States and in many other Western countries uses the criterion that the fetus should be able to survive by itself as the moment when abortion becomes illegal, what is sometimes referred to as the "point of viability." After this moment, abortion is not allowed for any reason. Debates about the gestational limits on abortion rage in the United States and differ from country to country. The U.S. court case *Roe v. Wade* legalized abortion under certain circumstances beyond twenty weeks, but not after the stage that the fetus is viable outside of the womb.

The Greek translation of Exodus 21:22–25 and its interpretation by Philo of Alexandria apply a different standard: whether or not the fetus is fully formed and the limbs are fully grown. It is not easy to pinpoint this to a particular moment, but all in all this seems to point at the sixteenth rather than the twentieth or even twenty-fourth week of a pregnancy. Application of the measure used in Exodus would in fact mean that the gestational limit on abortion should be put at around sixteen weeks.

In sum, the Bible is not very explicit about abortion. The sanctity of life is clearly asserted. However, Exodus 21:22–25 is the only passage in the entire Bible that explicitly deals with the fate of an unborn child. The Hebrew of this passage is rather ambiguous and may refer to the fate of the mother rather than to that of the fetus. The Greek version of the same passage does introduce a clear criterion: the question whether or not the fetus is fully formed. At the same time, however, Numbers 5:11–31 appears to contain instructions for the drinking of a potion that may cause infertility and perhaps even abortion. The same book, in 3:40, seems to imply that a baby was counted as a member among the Israelites only after a month of age. Given the silence of the New Testament on the subject of abortion, the only conclusion we can draw here is that the Bible is less outspoken in its verdict on abortion than might be expected.

For this reason, it is time to turn the attention to interpretive strategies for reading the instructions of especially Exodus 21:22–25. As will become clear in the final section of this essay, interpretations of this passage in early Christianity and among the early Jewish rabbis differed significantly. It is the difference between these interpretations that raises our final question: How should we interpret the biblical evidence today?

The authority of the Bible in early Christianity and early Judaism

Already in antiquity, the Bible's views of abortion gave rise to competing interpretations. The question that the Hebrew Bible left open—when does life begin?—was explicitly answered by Christian authors such as Athenagoras, Clement of Alexandria, Tertullian, and Lactantius. Their position is plain and simple: the human person is formed at the moment the soul enters the body and this happens at conception (Ricks 1992).

This conviction led to extreme positions. The second-century Christian text *Apocalypse of Peter*, sacred to some ancient Christians but not a part of the New Testament, contains a graphic detail which describes the punishment of women who practiced abortion: "And near this flame there is a pit, great and very deep, and into it flows from above all manner of torment, foulness, and excrement. And women are swallowed up therein up to their necks and tormented with great pain. These are they who have caused their children to be born untimely and have corrupted the work of God who created them" (Elliott 1993, 605, Ethiopic version). Apparently Christianity in its formative stage was so thoroughly concerned with taking a stand over against the practices of abortion and infanticide of the surrounding pagan cultures, that it translated this concern into this nightmarish vision. It undoubtedly served as a threat that should keep women from practicing abortion.

The Mishnah, a Jewish law code from around 200 C.E., and the Talmud, a later compilation of Jewish laws and interpretations of Scripture from around 500 C.E., both appear to use a stricter criterion than the instructions of Exodus 21:22–25. In the Mishnah, the moment the baby's head leaves the mother's body is seen as the moment life begins (see, e.g., m.Nid. 3:5 and m.Ohol. 7:6; Schiff 2004, 27–57). In this line of reasoning, which was continued in discussions in the Talmud, the focus is on the legal status of the person. For this reason the question of who should be seen as "a person" is of the utmost importance: "Given that the fetus was not designated as a *nefesh* or an *adam* (human) or an *ish* (man), and was, therefore, without any legal standing as a 'person', the category of murder was altogether inapplicable" (Schiff 2004, 28). This does not mean that abortion or feticide was allowed in early

Judaism—on the contrary, it was not—but it did lead to the idea that such a crime should be punished by a fine rather than a more severe punishment.

The authority of the Bible today

The different lines along which early Christians and Jews approached the matter of abortion still pose difficulties for Christians and Jews today who invoke the authority of the Bible to settle the debate on abortion. The decisive question in this debate seems to be the question of the formation of the human person: when does life begin?

Thus, the legal principle applied in early Judaism by the rabbis and the biological principle applied by the early Christian theologians arrive at different positions. Legally speaking, the unborn fetus cannot be seen as a human person. However, biologically the reverse seems true: far before birth the fetus moves and appears to behave as a person. In some early translations of Exodus 21:22–25, the condition of being fully formed in the physical sense is used as the point of no return in the consideration of personhood for a fetus.

In all their diversity, the writings collected as the Bible, be it in its Jewish or its Christian form, do indicate that life is to be preserved, at least from the moment onward that the child is recognizable as a human being. It is important to underline here, by the way, that especially in the Hebrew version of Exodus 21, the mother's life and well-being are taken as the prime focus of legislation: this certainly opens the possibility of negotiating an abortion in case the mother's health should be in serious danger.

One notable exception with regard to the preservation of life is explicitly addressed in the Book of Numbers, which concerns extramarital pregnancy (Num. 5:11–31). An adulteress should become infertile, and in case she should be pregnant, the fetus will not survive. The magical ritual that is prescribed there is so much determined by its historical context that the idea of reintroducing this practice would probably not find many adherents. A literal application of the biblical story does raise the question, however, of how to deal with pregnancies caused by rape. Choosing to ban abortion in cases where rape caused pregnancy would be difficult to argue as biblically supported, as the Book of Numbers prescribes a potion that should cause sterility and perhaps even abortion as the enforced consequence of infidelity. As a result, it is hard to argue that the Bible always speaks out against abortion.

All in all, the Bible does not speak as clearly about abortion as some politicians might wish. Where it does speak about pregnancy and abortion, the God-given character of human life is an important point of departure. On the one hand, there are passages that state how God has plans for some special human beings, his prophets, already during their stay in their mother's womb. This implies that already at that stage God had selected them as the persons they would become. On the other hand, some passages indicate that human life was only thought to begin either at the moment the fetus was fully developed or even up to a month after the baby's birth. It is therefore difficult to refer to anything like "the Bible's teaching on abortion." The Bible contains a diverse collection of views on the origin of human life. Any attempt to base a political strategy on the Bible should always indicate, for honesty's sake, that such a "biblical view" is based on a conscious choice of passages and interpretations by each individual speaker.

Works Cited

Ancient sources

Ancient authors are referred to in the translation of the *Loeb Classical Library* (Cambridge, MA: Harvard University Press; London: Heinemann), unless stated otherwise.

Cassuto, Umberto. *A Commentary on the Book of Genesis. Part One.* Jerusalem: The Magness Press, 1961.

Elliott, J.K. (ed.). *The Apocryphal New Testament: A Collection of Apocryphal Christian Literature in an English Translation based on M.R. James.* Oxford: Clarendon, 1993.

Flannagan, Matthew. "Feticide, the Masoretic Text, and the Septuagint." *Westminster Theological Journal* 74 (2012): 59–84.

Gnilka, Joachim. *Das Evangelium nach Markus (Mk 8,27–16,20).* Evangelisch-Katholischer Kommentar zum Neuen Testament II/2. Zürich: Benziger Verlag; Neukirchen-Vluyn: Neukirchener Verlag, 1979.

Goodnough, Abby. "Texas Abortion Law Has Women Waiting Longer, and Paying More." *The New York Times.* March 18, 2016.

Noort, Ed and Tigchelaar, Eibert (eds.). *The Sacrifice of Isaac: The Aqedah (Genesis 22) and Its Interpretations*. Themes in Biblical Narrative 4. Leiden: Brill, 2002.

Perkins, Larry J. "Exodus." In *New English Translation of the Septuagint*, edited by Albert Pietersma, Benjamin G. Wright, 43–81. Oxford, New York: Oxford University Press, 2009.

Ricks, Stephen D. "Abortion." In *Anchor Bible Dictionary*, edited by David Noel Freedman. Vol. 1, 31–35. New York: Doubleday, 1992.

Schiff, Daniel. *Abortion in Judaism*. Cambridge: Cambridge University Press, 2004.

Stern, Menachem (ed.). *Greek and Latin Authors on Jews and Judaism*. Vol. 2. Jerusalem: The Israel Academy of Sciences and Humanities, 1980.

Verhey, Allen. *Reading the Bible in the Strange World of Medicine*, 194–252, esp. ch. 6 "Abortion." Grand Rapids: Eerdmans, 2003.

Websites

Buncombe, Andrew. "Donald Trump Fluffs Bible Reference during Speech at Christian Liberty University." *Independent*. January 19, 2016. http://www.independent.co.uk/news/people/donald-trump-fluffs-bible -reference-in-speech-at-christian-liberty-university-a6819946.html (accessed January 22, 2016).

Johnson, Jenna. "Donald Trump Likes that Proverbs Verse that Might not Exist." *The Washington Post*. September 16, 2015. https://www .washingtonpost.com/news/post-politics/wp/2015/09/16/donald -trump-likes-that-proverbs-verse-that-might-not-exist/ (accessed March 8, 2016).

Minor, Jack. "Ted Cruz Calls Out Pastors to Fight Abortion." *WND*. August 25, 2015. http://www.wnd.com/2015/08/ted-cruz-calls-out -pastors-to-fight-abortion/ (accessed August 30, 2015).

Nededog, Jethro. "Stephen Colbert Calls Out Donald Trump for Apparent Bible Goof." *Business Insider UK*. January 22, 2016. http:// uk.businessinsider.com/colbert-donald-trump-bible-reading-2016 -1?r=US&IR=T (accessed January 25, 2016).

Scott, Eugene. "Marco Rubio Defends Abortion Stance: Human Life Begins at Conception." *CNN Politics*. August 7, 2015. http://iconosquare.com /p/1195213885749653849_10613643 (accessed March 3, 2016).

"Senator Ted Cruz on Abortion." *YouTube*, November 17, 2015. https:// www.youtube.com/watch?v=AlDnz4E9yf8 (accessed March 1, 2016).

Sherman, Amy. "Rubio Said He's Never Advocated for Abortion Exceptions for Rape or Incest." *Politifact*. August 7, 2015. http://www .politifact.com/florida/statements/2015/aug/07/marco-rubio/rubio-said -hes-never-advocated-abortion-exceptions/ (accessed August 30, 2015).

4

Senators, Snowballs, and Scripture: The Bible and Climate Change

Frances Flannery

By year's end, 2015 would prove to be the warmest year on record across the globe, after 2014 had just held that title. However, on February 26, 2015, it was so cold in Washington, D.C., that Senator James Inhofe (R–Oklahoma) brought a snowball onto the Senate floor during a debate on climate change. The most influential climate change denier in the Senate then declared, "… [B]ecause we keep hearing that 2014 has been the warmest year on record, I ask the Chair, you know what this is? It's a snowball. And that's just from outside here. So it's very, very cold out" (Mirsky 2015).

Senator Inhofe reasoned that because it was cold in D.C., global warming does not exist. Although Rhode Island Senator Sheldon Whitehouse (D–Rhode Island) followed Inhofe and refuted him with conclusions to the contrary drawn from NASA, the military, and the vast majority of scientists, his arguments did not sway Inhofe. He rebutted by asserting there was "archaeological," "historic," and "biblical evidence" that while the climate was changing, it was not because of humans (Schubman 2015). That day in the Senate, Whitehouse's amendment stating that climate change is real did pass, but a subsequent amendment which stated that climate change is "real" *and that human activity "contributes" to it* failed by just one vote. Only fifteen of fifty-four Republicans had voted in favor of that amendment which required sixty votes total to pass.

By contrast, 97 percent of climate scientists maintain that climate change is real and caused by human activity, particularly the production of greenhouse gases. They conclude that only drastic changes in our lifestyles can mitigate the grave effects of climate change, many of which are unavoidable and devastating, particularly to the poor. Depending on how quickly the great glaciers melt, scientists estimate that sea level will rise between 1.5 and 6.5 feet by the end of this century, displacing up to half a billion people and creating an unprecedented wave of "climate refugees" (IPCC 2014).

However, no amount of scientific evidence could sway Senator Inhofe because the "biblical evidence" that he mentioned is, for him and several politicians like him, the ultimate authority in deciding policy issues. These politicians interpret the Bible as saying that since God is the Creator who has control over the fate of the world, humans could not make changes so vast so as to influence the climate. Inhofe had recently made this clear in his 2012 book, *The Greatest Hoax: How the Global Warming Conspiracy Threatens Your Future*, in which he cites the Bible to support his rejection of scientific evidence that claims climate change is real. As he explains: "[T]he Genesis 8:22 that I use in [the book] is that 'as long as the earth remains there will be springtime, harvest, cold and heat, winter and summer, day and night.' My point is, God's still up there. The arrogance of people to think that we, human beings, would be able to change what He is doing in the climate is to me outrageous" (Eliason 2012).

Senator Inhofe's opinion matters not just by way of example, but because he was the Chair of the Senate Environment and Public Works Committee from 2003 to 2007, a position he has held again since 2015. With such an important role in shaping environmental policy for the United States and an admitted deference to the Bible on all matters, his interpretation of the Bible on climate change and other issues has real policy implications. For this reason, it is important to note that Inhofe has stated that climate change is actually only the "second largest hoax ever played on the American people after the separation of church and state" (Parkes 2013, 86).

Inhofe is far from alone in being a federal legislator whose opinions on science are preemptively shaped by his interpretation of the Bible. In both the Senate and the U.S. House of Representatives, public policy decisions on climate change and other scientific matters have been framed in terms of a choice between belief in biblical authority and God's authority, on the one hand, versus trust in science on the other. Representative Paul Broun (R–Georgia), who sits on the House Science, Space and Technology Committee, has openly stated, "God's Word is true," but evolution, embryology, and the Big Bang theory are "lies straight from the pit of Hell." As Broun promised, "The Bible...teaches us how to run all our public policy and everything in society. And that's the reason, as your congressman, I hold the Holy Bible as being the major directions to me of how I vote in Washington D.C., and I'll continue to do that" (Parkes 2013, 90; Pearce 2012).

At root for such politicians is a concern above all else to affirm God's power. Representative Ralph Moody Hall (R–Texas), Chair of the House Committee on Science, and Representative Joe Barton (R–Texas), the former Chair of the House Energy and Commerce Committee, both read the scientific evidence for climate change through this lens. As Barton argued about the increase in CO_2 in the atmosphere: "A lot of the CO_2 that is created in the United States is naturally created. You can't regulate God. Not even the Democratic majority in the US Congress can regulate God" (Parkes 2013, 88–89; Frick 2009; Mervis 2011).

This way of framing the climate change debate also shapes the platforms of many state and local level politicians. In North Carolina, all four Republican candidates for State Senate in 2014 answered the question, "Is climate change a fact?" with a flat "no," while one clarified, "God controls the climate" (Spross 2014).

Politicians mirror some trends present among the public. Fully 49 percent of Americans interpreted recent natural disasters as signs of "the biblical end times," a rapid 5 percent increase in just three years (PRRI 2014, 23). A recent survey found that white evangelical Protestants were more likely to interpret recent natural disasters (e.g., increased number and intensity of storms and flooding, as well as drought) as signs of the end times portrayed in the Bible (77 percent) rather than as effects of climate change (49 percent). By contrast, only 35 percent of white mainline Protestants and 43 percent of Catholics interpreted natural disasters as apocalyptic signs. And while 74 percent of black Protestants also viewed natural disasters as signs of the apocalypse, they were just as likely to also see these as signs of climate change (73 percent) (PRRI 2014, 23).

Thus, belief in the Bible does not necessarily mean denying that humans have caused climate change or that we bear a responsibility in mitigating its effects. The Evangelical Climate Initiative, a campaign by evangelical church leaders to promote mitigation of global warming, received little support until recently. Now it has gained the support of the National Association of Evangelicals, which represents thirty million church members (ECI 2015). The preamble testifies: "As American Evangelical Christian Leaders, we recognize both our opportunity and our responsibility to offer a *biblically based moral witness* that can help shape public policy in the most powerful nation on earth, and therefore contribute to the well-being of the entire world" (ECI 2015).

Similarly, Pope Francis, who obviously considers the Bible to be a moral and social authority, recently issued a massive encyclical on climate change subtitled "On Care for Our Common Home," calling for mitigation (Pope Francis 2015). Jewish leaders have also advocated for active environmentalism, finding their mandate in readings of Genesis 1–2 and the Jewish concept of *Tikkun Olam*, humankind's partnership with the divine in repairing a broken world (JCI 2009, 13).

Clearly, there is a huge diversity of opinion on whether the Bible supports or denies climate change and environmental activism. Biblical scholarship can contribute to the debate by shedding some light on the original meanings of the verses that politicians and pundits typically cite for or against mitigation and the existence of human induced climate change.

Genesis 8:22 and climate change

The Bible stresses that God has control over the weather. Without a doubt, the Bible—both the Hebrew Bible or Old Testament and the New Testament—portrays God as the Creator of our world with power to influence its operations, such as the movement of the sun and the moon (e.g., Gen. 1:14–18).

What Senator Inhofe calls his "favorite passage" reads: "As long as the earth endures, seedtime and harvest, cold and heat, summer and winter, day and night, shall not cease" (Gen. 8:22). The verse appears at the conclusion of the flood story, in which everything with the breath of life perishes, except for Noah, his family, and the animals on the ark. Thus, after a devastating disaster, the phrase promises that the most basic cycles of nature will continue, as in the proverbial phrase "the sun always rises."

However, Genesis 8:22 *never* promises there will no longer be severe storms, that the "cold and heat" won't be more extreme, or that God will prevent humans from wreaking destruction. It does not promise that God will clean up our messes, save animals from wrongful human activity, or even preserve our species. The Book of Genesis elsewhere suggests that humans have free will and that the consequences of our poor choices are left to stand (e.g., Gen. 4:7–10). Moreover, the larger context of the flood story asserts that God can always regret his actions and change God's mind, so that continued human existence is not an inalienable right.

According to Genesis, God punished the world by global flooding because "every inclination of the thoughts of [humans'] hearts was only evil continually. And the LORD was sorry that he had made humankind on the earth, and it grieved him to his heart" (Gen. 6:5–7). God's sorrow and regret extended to the whole creation: "[T]he earth was filled with violence. And God saw that the earth was corrupt; for all flesh had corrupted its ways upon the earth" (Gen. 6:11–12).

The point is that Genesis maintains human violence on the earth was so great that it spread to *the very earth and animals*. That's a pretty strong statement about humans' ability to impact the world, which is typically the position that biblically based climate change deniers wish to deny.

Historical criticism, a methodology that compares the flood story in Genesis with contemporary ancient Near Eastern flood stories, can shed even more light on the worldview of the Genesis text. *The Epic of Gilgamesh* predates the composition of Genesis by at least a thousand years and contains a similar flood story. Like Genesis, *Gilgamesh* also has angry gods who wish to wipe out humans, a god (Ea) who has a favorite human (Utnapishtim) whom

he tells to build a boat, and gods who unleash a devastating flood
that kills all the humans and animals on earth except for those on
the boat.

Similarly to Noah in Genesis, Utnapishtim releases birds after the
mighty rains to see how far the flood has subsided. He begins with
a dove, which fails to find a perch, and progresses to the farther
roaming swallow, which also fails. The last bird he releases is a
raven, which eats, caws with delight, and does not return since it
has all the raven food it desires—the floating corpses of the majority
of humans and animals on earth (Sandars 1986, 111).

Genesis 8 seems to know this story, but makes a significant
change. Noah releases the raven while the waters are still high
and it goes "to and fro," perhaps hopping from corpse to corpse
(Gen. 8:7). But then Noah releases a dove, which brings back an
olive leaf to show that nature has rebounded. Noah then releases
the dove again and it does not return. Its permanent absence shows
it has found enough grain and fruit to subsist on (Gen. 8:10–12).
Thus, the biblical story ends not with the raven but with the dove,
an image of a rebounding natural world. The small change in order
of the birds signals that Genesis has hope.

The context for Genesis 8:22, then, is the story of a global
ecosystem (plants, animals, earth, and humans) that is devastated
with climate tragedy on account of human sin and that rebounds
afterward with a greatly reduced animal population.

Specifically, Genesis 8:22 pledges that the basic cycles of nature
will continue through a series of promises. God states He will
never again "curse the *ground* (*adamah* in Hebrew) because of
humankind (*adam*), for the inclination of the human heart is evil
from youth" (Gen. 8:21). He will never engage in extermination of
"every living creature" (Gen. 8:21). He will never again destroy all
flesh or the earth with a flood (Gen. 9:10–11).

The promise is made to Noah and his children, namely that
the human species will continue with a handful of people. But
this contract is also made with "every living creature that is with
you [Noah], the birds, the domestic animals, and every animals"
(Gen. 9:10–11). That is, God promises not to destroy *all* animals
on earth or the entire earth itself as punishment for humankind's
wickedness, which is not to say that God would not destroy these in
part. At maximum, Genesis 8:22 and the passages around it promise
that the seasons will alternate, that day and night will continue,

and that at least *some* life on earth will continue as long as the earth continues. The passage does not speak to the issue of whether humans could cause catastrophic changes to the global ecosystem.

Genesis 1:28 and human dominion over the earth

Sometimes, politicians bring up Genesis 1:28 to refute climate change mitigation efforts, such as curbing CO_2 emissions or greenhouse gases. This verse quotes God giving a mission to humankind: "Be fruitful and multiply, and fill the earth and subdue it; and have dominion over the fish of the sea and over the birds of the air and over every living thing that moves upon the earth." Some take this to mean that humans can do whatever they wish to the earth and its animals, justifying the rejection of climate change proposals that would impact our economy or way of life. As Rick Santorum, former Pennsylvania Senator and 2012 and 2016 Presidential Candidate, explains: "We were put on this Earth as creatures of God to have dominion over the Earth, to use it wisely and steward it wisely, but for our benefit, not for the Earth's benefit" (Lacey 2012).

In fact, the larger literary context of the verse seems to indicate that our role is to take care of the earth. In this first creation story in Genesis, humans are the last created creatures, the pinnacle of creation (as opposed to the next creation story in Genesis 2:4–24, in which we are created before any other animals exist). God proclaims all of the animals to be "good," even creeping things and "sea monsters" (Gen. 2:21, 25). It is an ideal creation, in which nothing bad exists.

Using the lens of historical criticism, we see that Genesis 1 is radical in comparison to many ancient Near Eastern creation stories, which almost always portray creation as coming out of destruction and violence. For instance, in the older and more widely circulated Babylonian *Enuma Elish*, the dome of heaven is created out of the severed half of the primordial sea entity that is the mother of all the gods. By contrast, Genesis uses a word meaning "a hammered sheet of tin" to describe the creation of the dome of heaven (Gen. 1:6). Throughout Genesis 1, God creates with no destruction and repeatedly sees that it is "good."

Since humans are created "in the image of God" (Gen. 1:27) and up to this point God only creates and sustains a remarkably good world, it appears that we too are meant to be creative, not destructive. Thus, the command to "subdue" the earth cannot mean to wreck it and "have dominion" cannot mean to exploit the animals for our benefit. In fact, the very next verse explains that humans are created to be totally vegetarian: "God said, 'See, I have given you every plant yielding seed that is upon the face of all the earth, and every tree with seed in its fruit; you shall have them for food'" (Gen. 1:29). This food system and the whole world are said to be "very good" (Gen. 1:31).

The Hebrew word translated "subdue," *kavash*, is used elsewhere in the Bible to mean bring a land under control (Num. 32:22; 1 Chr. 22:18; and Micah 7:19) (although it can have some violent connotations as well in other passages). The word translated "to have dominion," *mashal*, literally means "to rule"—the same verb that describes how the sun rules over the day (Gen. 1:16). Hence, if the first chapter of Genesis is fairly coherent, Genesis 1:28 seems to indicate that God commands the human creature to rule *in the same creative, non-destructive manner* over the animals and earth as God has ruled over the world.

The Book of Revelation

When 49 percent of Americans interpret natural disasters as signs of the apocalypse, they are likely drawing on impressions gleaned from the Book of Revelation. This apocalyptic reading anticipates a final series of end-time events that includes periodic and partial devastations to the earth and its inhabitants, some vaguely reminiscent of environmental devastation. As a biblical scholar, I read these passages in their original historical context, namely, as the visionary experiences of a seer, John of Patmos, living at the end of the first century C.E./A.D. under the oppressive Roman Emperor Domitian. His visions convey a nonhistorical time in the future during which all evil (the Roman Empire and its allies, ultimately ruled by Satan) is defeated.

As John's visions unfold, a series of symbols conveys the successive punishments of God that are being cast upon the earth, often resulting in environmental destruction. In one vision, angels blow trumpets that release hail, fire, and blood onto the earth that burn up a third of the earth, trees, and grass; another angel hurls fire into the sea that kills a third of the creatures; and another strikes out a third of the light of the sun, moon, and stars (Rev. 8:7–12). In a later vision, angels pour out seven golden bowls of wrath (Rev. 15:7): "The fourth angel poured his bowl on the sun, and it was allowed to scorch people with fire; they were scorched by the fierce heat" (Rev. 16:8–9). Some modern apocalyptic readers interpret this as global warming, which they then conclude is divinely made.

The culmination of all these plagues is judgment on Babylon, a symbol for Rome (see Rev. 17:9, which identifies the city as sitting on seven hills). After a series of other battles (Armageddon, and Gog and Magog), the global end-time arrives. The earth passes away, a new earth appears, and the heavenly Jerusalem descends from heaven to the new earth. It has no weather at all, because there is no sun or moon (Rev. 21:1–14, 23).

Since the visions in Revelation are given in symbolic form, many have interpreted them to fit current events of their time. Countless times in medieval Europe colorful preachers used the Book of Revelation to interpret astronomical and weather signs to calculate the Second Coming on a certain date, sometimes using this information to mobilize mob violence or crusades. In early America, the Millerites drew on Revelation to understand a blazing comet that appeared from February 28 to April 1, 1843, as signaling that Christ would return that year. When this did not occur, they recalculated and set the date again in 1844, according to scriptural clues. Despite a long history of failed predictions, some readers will continue to believe they are living in the time to which the Book of Revelation refers.

However, modern readers who take this position must ignore the historical context provided by the Book of Revelation itself. The book is addressed as letters to seven churches in ancient Asia Minor or Turkey, naming specific events at the end of the first century during the time of the Roman Empire (Rev. 2:1–3:22; Bauckham 1993, 13, 19). Since the book ends with Jesus saying, "See, I am coming soon!," those applying the fourth bowl of wrath to climate change must insert thousands of years into this timeline.

The Bible on the weather, earth, and human causation of climate change: A covenantal view

The Bible does not address contemporary climate change directly. However, the Bible *does* speak of vast weather changes and the decimation of animal and plant life on earth. It links these to human activity—Israel's failure to observe the Mosaic covenant, the laws given in Exodus, Leviticus, Numbers, and Deuteronomy. From the beginning of the creation of *adam* (human) out of *adamah* (ground) (Gen. 2:7), the Bible depicts an intimate relationship between the two. Humans might best be called "earthlings," in light of the Hebrew word play.

The covenant asserts that when Israel obeys God, the earth flourishes with abundant rain, a favorable climate, and fertility for animals, humans, and agriculture. Conversely, when Israel disobeys, punishing drought, devastation, and infertility will ensue (Deut. 28:11–12, 17–18, 23–24). Many of the prophets presume that this covenantal mechanism explains how the world operates. For example, consider how Hosea links human immorality with environmental devastation:

> Swearing, lying, and murder and stealing and adultery break out; bloodshed follows bloodshed. Therefore the land mourns, and all who live in it languish. Together with the wild animals and the birds of the air, even the fish of the sea are perishing. (Hosea 4:2–3)

Yet, while numerous biblical passages make a connection between human activity and climate change, it is not in the modern sense. In the Bible it is human sin, not our technology and lifestyle, that changes the patterns of nature.

Reflections

Upon inspection, the biblical verses cited by climate change deniers do not support their policy positions. The Bible does not claim that human behavior cannot affect the earth on a vast scale; on the contrary, the flood story and scattered passages about God's covenant with Israel all maintain that humankind's sin can negatively impact the entire earth and its creatures. Genesis also lays responsibility for the welfare of the earth significantly on the shoulders of humankind, as God's representative. However, to be fair, the Bible also never envisions global climate change as a state induced through humankind's technological developments and consumptive lifestyle. Some texts anticipate God eventually replacing the earth with another, better one—a possible argument against costly environmental mitigation.

In the interest of transparency, my interpretations come with a disclaimer. I am a biblical scholar today, but my career began as an environmental scientist. At the end of the 1980s, I was already hearing grim news about climate change in my college environmental geology and ecology courses. Without a doubt, my personal position accepts the findings of 97 percent of the world's leading climate scientists that climate change is real and caused primarily by human activity.

I have carefully studied the reasons why climate scientists estimate that the impacts of climate change will include an increase in extreme weather events, serious drought in some areas and severe flooding in others, more intense storms and heat waves, increased health risks, destruction of coral reefs, forest death in the Rockies, longer wildfire seasons, melting ice, stress on food systems, pressure on groundwater supplies, habitat decimation, and the demise of massive amounts of species (but not of all life on earth) (IPCC 2014). As a former environmental scientist, this chain of events makes sense to me.

I have struggled to determine whether my personal commitments to environmental activism have influenced my interpretations *as a biblical scholar*. Here as elsewhere, I try hard to let the text speak regardless of whether I "like" the answer or not. Since there is textual evidence for my conclusions and I have carefully used the methods of biblical scholarship, my environmental leanings have led me to notice the nonhuman actors in the Bible a bit more than some interpreters, leading to a less human-centered reading. I have noticed that the Hebrew Bible often places great attention on the well-being of the earth, animals, and plants.

Thus, my hope is that biblical scholarship can provoke those who base their policy opinions on the Bible to think more clearly about what it really says. Personally, however, I do not think that we should ever form public policy based on the Bible, even when some passages happen to agree with my personal politics. Rather, I see a cautionary tale embedded in the well-meaning words of Representative Nancy Pelosi (D–California), minority leader of the House and Former Speaker of the House. She released an April 22 Earth Day press announcement, stating: "The Bible tells us in the Old Testament, 'To minister to the needs of God's creation is an act of worship. To ignore those needs is to dishonor the God who made us'" (Winn 2008). I really like this sentiment. Unfortunately, this biblical verse does not exist.

Works Cited

Barker, David C. and Bearce, David H. "End-Times Theology, the Shadow of the Future, and Public Resistance to Addressing Global Climate Change." *Political Research Quarterly* 66 (2013): 267–279.

Bauckham, Richard J. *The Theology of the Book of Revelation.* Cambridge: Cambridge University Press, 1993.

Eliason, Vic. Interview with Senator James Inhofe. Voice of Christian Youth America. March 7, 2012.

Environmental Climate Initiative. *Preamble and Statement.* Academy of Evangelical Scientists and Ethicists. 2015.

Frick, A. "Barton: We Shouldn't Regulate CO2 because 'It's in Your Coca-Cola' and 'You Can't Regulate God.'" *Climate Progress.* 2009.

Haller, Jessica, Savage, Nigel and Sinclair, Yedidya. "Sustaining Our Vision: The Jewish Climate Change Campaign." Alliance for Religions and Conservation. November 2009.

Inhofe, James. *The Greatest Hoax: How the Global Warming Conspiracy Threatens Your Future.* Washington, D.C.: WND Books, 2012.

IPCC, Intergovernmental Panel on Climate Change, 2014: Summary for Policymakers. In *Climate Change 2014: Mitigation of Climate Change. Contribution of Working Group III to the Fifth Assessment Report of the Intergovernmental Panel on Climate Change*, edited by O. Edenhofer, R. Pichs-Madruga, Y. Sokona, E. Farahani, S. Kadner, K. Seyboth, A. Adler, I. Baum, S. Brunner, P. Eickemeier, B. Kriemann, J. Savolainen, S. Schlömer, C. von Stechow, T. Zwickel, and J.C. Minx. Cambridge: Cambridge University Press, 2014.

Jewish Climate Change Campaign. *Sustaining Our Vision: Document for Alliance of Religions and Conservation Celebration at Windsor Castle.* 2009. http://www.arcworld.org/downloads/Jewish-CCC-7YP.pdf (accessed March 19, 2016).

Lacey, Steven. "Santorum's Incoherence." *Climate Progress*. February 7, 2012.

Mervis, J. "Ralph Hall Speaks Out on Climate Change." *Science Insider*. December 14, 2011.

Mirsky, Steve. "Climate Skeptic Senator Burned after Failed Snowball Stunt." *Scientific American*. March 2, 2015.

Parkes, Graham. "The Politics of Global Warming (2): Two Obstacles to Circumvent." In *Environmental Philosophy: The Art of Life in a World of Limits*, edited by Liam Leonard, John Barry, Marius de Geus, Peter Doran, and Graham Parkes, 81–110. Bingley: Emerald, 2013.

Pearce, Matt. "U.S. Rep. Paul Broun: Evolution a Lie 'from the pit of hell.'" *Los Angeles Times*. October 7, 2012.

Pope Francis. "Encyclical Letter: Laudato Si'." *The Vatican*. May 24, 2015. http://w2.vatican.va/content/francesco/en/encyclicals/documents/papa -francesco_20150524_enciclica-laudato-si.html (accessed May 25, 2015).

PRRI. "Why Americans Are Conflicted about Climate Change, Environmental Policy, and Science." November 21, 2014. http:// publicreligion.org/research/2014/11/believers-sympathizers-skeptics -americans-conflicted-climate-change-environmental-policy-science/# .VtTMkinednI (accessed November 26, 2014).

Sandars, Nancy K. (trans.). *The Epic of Gilgamesh: An English Version with an Introduction*. New York: Penguin, 1986 [1960].

Shubman, Jerry. "Watch a US Senator Cite the Bible to Prove That Humans Aren't Causing Global Warming." *Mother Jones*. January 22, 2015.

Spross, Jeff. "All Four of North Carolina's GOP Senate Candidates Are Climate Deniers." *Climate Progress*. April 23, 2014.

Winn, Pete. "Biblical Scholars Challenge Pelosi's 'Scripture' Quote." U.S. Senate Committee on Environment and Public Works. April 23, 2008.

5

Work, Poverty, and Welfare

Rodney A. Werline

The House Committee and 2 Thessalonians 3:10 and Matthew 25:31–46

During the House Committee on Agriculture debate in May 2013, both Republicans and Democrats took to quoting Bible verses at one another. The Republican bill under discussion proposed drastic cuts to the Supplemental Nutrition Assistance Program (SNAP)— the "food stamps" program in popular speech. According to the *New York Times* "The Caucus," a blog on politics and government, Rep. Juan C. Vargas (D–California) quoted Jesus's words from Matthew 25 and directed them at the Republicans who supported cutting the program (Nixon 2013). "I'm a Christian," Rep. Vargas asserted, "and this chapter talks about how you treat the least among us" (Nixon 2013). Disagreement then erupted over whether Jesus expected governments or individuals to offer assistance to the poor. Rep. Stephen Fincher (R–Tennessee) responded with a quote from Matthew 26:11: "For you always have the poor with you" (Nixon 2013). According to another blog and opinion column, Rep. Fincher also justified the cuts to the programs with 2 Thessalonians 3:10: "For even when we were with you, we gave you this command: Anyone unwilling to work should not eat" (Ungar 2013).

Rep. Fincher is a Tea Party Republican, a conservative, and an evangelical Christian. Unsurprisingly, his use of 2 Thessalonians occurs frequently in sermons and debates from the Christian right in opposition to welfare and other kinds of government assistance for the poor. Especially notorious among this group is John Hagee, a fundamentalist megachurch minister in San Antonio, Texas, also known for claiming that hurricane Katrina was the result of God's punishment on gays. Hagee is fixated on the end of the world and preaches that the rapture and tribulation period will happen soon, focusing in particular on the role of the modern state of Israel in the events leading to the end. Hagee's attack on those who are "able-bodied" but not working appears in links on right-wing sites and can be easily found on YouTube:

> We [America] became great by every American getting off his duff, getting himself a job, and making his life a thing of beauty based on his own efforts. To those of you who are sick, to those of you who are elderly, to those of you who are disabled, we gladly support you. To the healthy who can work but won't work, get your nasty self off the couch [yelling] and go get a job!...America has rewarded laziness and we have called it welfare. The Bible says, "The man who does not work, should not eat." I know the liberals hate that verse, but read it and weep! It's God's position! (*RWW News* 2014)

However, for many biblical scholars, a reading of this passage in 2 Thessalonians is not quite as simple as it is for Rep. Fincher and John Hagee. In fact, interpretations of 2 Thessalonians 3 are fraught with complications. The verse is not easily applied to a contemporary setting, including using it as a proof-text verse to argue against SNAP. First, many biblical scholars doubt that Paul wrote this New Testament document, even though it bears his name. The problem of authorship centers in part on 2 Thessalonians's ideas about the end of the world, which do not match Paul's other letters. In 1 Thessalonians, for example, Paul seems to think that the end of time and Jesus's return could happen at any moment (1 Thess. 5:1–11). The author of 2 Thessalonians, however, tells his readers that the end of time is not close and that several events must take place before the end can come. Thus, critical scholars believe that the author of 2 Thessalonians pushes the end further into the future because the end did not come as the real, historical Paul had predicted (see Ehrman 2015).

If the text was probably not written by Paul, what is the problem in 2 Thessalonians and how does it relate to work? 2 Thessalonians is written by someone in the early church to people in the church; the problem is an intra-church matter and not part of a fight about a government program. The letter may be dealing with people who have quit their jobs because they think that Jesus is about to return. Why work when the end is near? It would be like having the knowledge that you are about to win the lottery—time to quit! However, as we know, the end they had expected did not come immediately. Though these people maintained their fanatical fervor, they still needed to eat. Most likely, they began to rely on people who had continued to work for their food. Or, they may have imposed on the generosity of the wealthy members of the congregation. The tensions and conflicts must have grown by the time 2 Thessalonians was written.

Church members behaving in this way would have been an embarrassment within Roman culture and it could only have complicated that church's already difficult situation. Within Roman culture, a person who quit working in order to be completely dedicated to a particular deity, especially a "new" deity from a distant land like Judea and Galilee, would be considered fanatical and superstitious. This idea is difficult for many modern Christians to grasp. The Romans, who believed that certain people could find answers through examining entrails of sacrificed animals or chickens pecking grain, seem like a superstitious group to modern Christians. For the author of 2 Thessalonians, the early church had enough problems in that society as it was; the members did not need to add a criticism of sloth. While we do not know the extent of the persecution at the time of writing 2 Thessalonians, whether it was government-sponsored oppression or local social pressure, the letter indicates that the people are suffering.

When discussing work and welfare in a modern setting, 2 Thessalonians may have little relevance. That text is about people who have given up work for a fanatical religious belief that the end is near at the turn of the first century C.E. We live in a democratic government with a capitalistic economic system that is tied into complex global markets. Actually, I am not confident that 2 Thessalonians offers anything to the current political discussion and it should not be invoked to support a government policy.

Equally problematic is the interpretation of Matthew 25, the text cited by Rep. Vargas in support of SNAP in May 2013. In this chapter, I can only refer to a few of these problems, but there are many more.

The passage in Matthew is a favorite of many socially left-leaning individuals—both theological liberals and socially liberal evangelicals, such as Jim Wallis of *Sojourners* (Doerer). In general, these socially liberal interpreters read the passage much like Rep. Vargas, that Matthew's Jesus teaches that *all* people will be judged on how they treat the poor who live among them—"the least of these." But, could the text mean something different from this?

Actually, it might.

In the scene in Matthew 25:31–46, Jesus speaks about the judgment of the "nations" (*ethné*), as most Bibles translate the term. The alternate meaning of the term is "Gentiles," non-Jews, which is often overlooked by translators. The author may have in mind a judgment of the Gentile kingdoms that will take place at the end of time (Harrington 1991). Earlier in Matthew, Jesus told the disciples that they would judge Israel—the Jews—as they sit upon twelve thrones: "Jesus said to them, 'Truly I tell you, at the renewal of all things, when the Son of Man is seated on the throne of his glory, you who have followed me will also sit on twelve thrones, judging the twelve tribes of Israel'" (Matt. 19:28). Matthew, then, may think that there will be two different judgments—one for Israel and one for Gentile kingdoms.

A figure called the Son of Man "comes in his glory" to begin the judgment in Matthew 25. This figure appears in other texts from that era and takes a key role in other end-of-time judgment scenes, for example, in Daniel 7. Who gathers the Gentile nations in Matthew is not clear, though it may be the angels. Matthew depicts those who are to be judged as sheep and goats. The sheep are placed on the right-hand side of king (whose identity is a bit of a problem) and the goats to his left. The sheep are then granted access to the "kingdom" because they gave care to "the king" in moments of distress, as the king says:

[F]or I was hungry and you gave me food, I was thirsty and you gave me something to drink, I was a stranger and you welcomed me, I was naked and you gave me clothing, I was sick and you took care of me, I was in prison and you visited me. (Matt. 25:35–36)

The sheep are surprised because they do not remember seeing the king in these situations and they ask when they performed these acts for the king:

The king then responds: "Truly I tell you, just as you did it to one of the least of these who are members of my family, you did it to me." (Matt 25:40)

The goats on the king's left, however, are told that they did not help the king in difficult circumstances. Like the sheep, they are puzzled over when they saw the king like this, but abandoned him. The king replies to them:

Truly I tell you, just as you did not do it to one of the least of these, you did not do it to me. (Matt. 25:45)

The goats are then sent off to "eternal punishment" (Matt. 25:46).

Who are "the least of these" with whom the king identifies? Notice that the New Revised Standard Version translates the phrase this way: "the least of these who are members of my family." Other versions translate this phrase as "these least of these my brothers." In popular interpretations, the "least of these" is interpreted as the poor in general. With this understanding, then, the king gives entry into the kingdom to anyone who has helped the downtrodden.

However, in Matthew, references to people in the diminutive, like "the little ones," generally refer to the disciples who follow Jesus (Harrington 1991). The passages that best demonstrate this are Matthew 18:6 and 10: "If any of you put a stumbling block before one of these little ones who believe in me"; and "Take care that you do not despise one of these little ones; for, I tell you, in heaven their angels continually see the face of my Father in heaven." The diminutive language in chapter 25 may have the same force—the "least of these my brothers" may very well refer to the followers of Jesus. This identification finds further support from a text in which Jesus asks, "Who is my mother, and who are my brothers?" He answers his own question by pointing to his disciples and identifying them as his family: "And pointing to his disciples, he said, 'Here are my mother and my brothers! For whoever does the will of my Father in heaven is my brother and sister and mother'" (Matt. 12:48–50).

If we identify the "nations" as Gentile kingdoms and the "least of these" as the followers of Jesus, the meaning of the text changes considerably. Now the text claims that the Gentile kingdoms will be judged on how they treated the followers of Jesus. As a result, once again, application of the passage in a twenty-first-century context in any direct manner becomes difficult.

So, two biblical passages often quoted by both sides of the work–welfare debate prove to be more complicated than is often assumed. As a result, casting these texts into a modern debate about policy for a democratic capitalistic society seems quite problematic.

However, does the Bible contain texts that expect, exhort, value, or praise work? Certainly! Are there biblical passages that express concern about the poor? Absolutely! As we might expect, these passages also possess their own unique interpretation problems. Nevertheless, I will scan through a few of these texts.

Overview of the Bible on work and poverty

Perhaps the Book of Proverbs contains the most statements about the importance of work. Proverbs constantly warns of the dangers of laziness (Prov. 10:26; 12:24, 27; 13:4; 15:19; 19:24; 20:4; 21:25; 22:13; 24:30; 26:13–16). While the history of the construction and editing of this book is quite complex, the writing most likely embodies the instructions of ancient wise men who taught the sons of the Jerusalem elite. Expectedly, the sayings reflect the perspective of the wealthy, and they seem, in general, to oversimplify the reasons for poverty. For Proverbs, laziness is the cause of poverty: "A slack hand causes poverty, but the hand of the diligent makes rich" (Prov. 10:4). Because ancient Israel and Judah had an agricultural economy, the text speaks about laziness and poverty from that perspective: "The lazy person does not plow in season;

harvest comes, and there is nothing to be found" (Prov. 20:4). In an agrarian setting, work can be a matter of life and death. The person who does not plant, tend, and harvest will starve. Further, much of the agricultural work required a community of people. Thus, the person who did not work could also put others at risk. If that lazy person later expected help from others, people would naturally grow angry and frustrated with that individual.

Still, the ancient sages in Proverbs could encourage compassion toward the poor as a religious obligation: "The poor are disliked even by their neighbors, but the rich have many friends. Those who despise their neighbors are sinners, but happy are those who are kind to the poor" (Prov. 14:20–21; 19:7). Then, a few lines later a teacher warns: "Those who oppress the poor insult their Maker, but those who are kind to the needy honor him" (Prov. 14:31; cf. 17:5; 22:9). God rewards those who help the poor: "Whoever is kind to the poor lends to the LORD, and will be repaid in full" (Prov. 19:17). Several of the proverbs seem to instruct the students, if they have a future opportunity, to be careful to defend the just cause of the poor in the courts (Prov. 21:13; 22:16, 22–23). The wealthy should protect the rights of the poor (Prov. 31:9; Hoppe 2009). This may also suggest that their views of the causes of poverty are more complex than simple laziness, but we do not hear lengthy elaborations on those causes.

As in many societies, a significant disconnect may have existed between the very wealthy and the very poor in ancient Israel. We might get a taste of this problem from Ecclesiastes. This book also arises from wealthy elite teachers. The author of Ecclesiastes is filled with anxiety about how death threatens to rob life of all meaning. For this author, work provides a partial antidote to this threat. Work creates a buffer, if only temporarily, against despair: "There is nothing better for mortals than to eat and drink, and find enjoyment in their toil. This also, I saw, is from the hand of God..." (Eccl. 2:24–25). The writer worries about his projects, his power, and his wealth. At one point, he projects contentment and calm upon the labor class, and assumes that they have many fewer worries because they do not have to worry about their wealth. Therefore, they must sleep well at night: "Sweet is the sleep of laborers, whether they eat little or much; but the surfeit of the rich will not let them sleep" (Eccl. 5:12). While we do not have their voices, the poor laborers might say that they would gladly exchange places with the author.

The Torah, the first five books of the Hebrew Bible/Christian Old Testament, makes special provisions for the poor. For example, interest may not be extracted from the Israelite poor. Further, if a person has become so indebted to another Israelite that the person only has a coat as a possession to use collateral on a loan, the lender must return the coat at the end of the day (Exod. 22:25–27 and Deut. 24:12–13). Leviticus provided a kind of security net for the poor in their directions about harvesting fields (Lev. 19:9–11). When harvesting, landowners were not to go back over the fields or to harvest to the edges, but were to leave this surplus for the poor. Deuteronomy includes similar rules regarding leaving food for the alien, orphan, and widow (Deut. 24:19–21). According to Exodus, every seventh year the people were to allow the fields to lay fallow. Whatever grew in the fields naturally during that year was left for the poor (Exod. 23: 10–11; cf. Lev. 25:3–7). Deuteronomy also sets in place regulations that secure proper and prompt payment to the poor for their labor (Deut. 24:14–15; cf. Isa. 58:3 and Mal. 3:5).

While these texts are sometimes cited as indications of sensitivity to the needs of the poor, a person might still wonder if these rules actually go far enough. Could more or something different have been done for the poor? One scholar even thinks that some of these regulations may even have been put in place with the interests of the wealthy in mind (Bennett 2002). The potential inadequacy of these laws becomes visible in the book of Ruth, whose plot draws, in part, on some of these regulations. Ruth, a foreigner—a Moabite, comes to Israel with her Israelite mother-in-law, Naomi. Both are recent widows. Naomi must depend on Ruth to work in the fields in the company of the poor who are going behind the harvesters and gathering what they miss and leave behind (Ruth 2). This is a difficult existence. Class lines between rich and poor are everywhere in the story, and the dangers of being a poor woman working like this in the field become apparent. If a woman like this were assaulted, would she find an advocate? Ruth is not attacked, but she does find an advocate, whom she eventually marries. But what if Naomi did not have Ruth to work for her? How would Naomi survive if she could not work in the field?

The Psalms also contain many references to "the poor." While sometimes a metaphor for every person who understands her or his dependence on God, in several passages "the poor" functions as a socioeconomic category. One of the best examples occurs in Psalm 72:

> May he defend the cause of the poor of the people, give deliverance to the needy, and crush the oppressor (v. 4).… For he delivers the needy when they call, the poor and those who have no helper. He has pity on the weak and the needy, and saves the lives of the needy. From oppression and violence he redeems their life; and precious is their blood in his sight. (vv. 4, 12–14)

Even if "the poor" has become a metaphor to refer to the righteous, the text nevertheless attests that people sensed that they had obligations to the poor and their needs.

While some of the texts we have discussed were disappointing because they did not adequately explore the ways in which people become impoverished, several of ancient Israel's prophets do address this. Some of them view poverty as the result of the wealthy and powerful stacking the economic deck against the poor. This critique of society especially appears in Amos, Isaiah, and Micah. The traditions in these books, while clearly edited and updated, have roots in the eighth century B.C.E. In this system, the wealthy elites controlled the markets and lending money. Therefore, they could drive down the price of grain when it is sold at market. The grain prices leave the farmers unable to pay for the loans they had taken out to plant the crop. Interest payments on the loans also may have been exorbitant. When the farmers defaulted, the wealthy foreclosed on their lands being held as collateral and seized them. Besides the immorality of the process itself, the taking of land in this way may have also offended the notion of land ownership in Judah and Israel. For some, land was not capital that could be sold and moved, but a divinely given inheritance to a particular tribe and family. The land was to remain in the family.

In the Gospels, Jesus does not teach about a work ethic. In his parables and some of his sayings, we encounter such workers as farmers, shepherds, fishermen, day laborers, and servants. However, Jesus's concern about the poor and those being oppressed by imperial power is unmistakable. Many scholars who attempt to reconstruct an image of the historical Jesus believe that he hoped for the coming renewal of the people of Israel and the realization of the prophets' visions of economic justice (e.g., Horsley 1993). Jesus was the special agent of that renewal. He may have been especially concerned about poor laborers who eked out a livelihood at a subsistence level as well as the destitute. Their condition resulted from cooperation between the Romans and the Jerusalem ruling elite, who grew rich from this association. Jesus called that just order "the Kingdom of God." That Kingdom certainly included the poor and those forced to the margins. Many Gospel traditions preserve this feature of Jesus's ideas, but here we present only a few.

In a scene that Matthew and Luke share, Jesus tells messengers from John the Baptist that his mission to the poor is a sign that Jesus is the one sent from God: "Jesus answered them, 'Go and tell John [the Baptist] what you hear and see: the blind receive their sight, the lame walk, the lepers are cleansed, the deaf hear, the dead are raised, and *the poor have good news brought to them*'" (Matt. 11:4–5, parallel Luke 7:22).

The Gospel of Luke exhibits special interest in the plight of the poor. Luke's version of the "beatitudes" comes with a set of corresponding "woes" in which the poor are blessed and the rich are cursed:

> Blessed are you who are poor, for yours is the kingdom of God.
> Blessed are you who are hungry now, for you will be filled....
> But woe to you who are rich, for you have received your consolation.
> Woe to you who are full now, for you will be hungry. (Luke 6: 20–21, 24–25)

In Luke's telling of Jesus's story about a great wedding banquet, the poor become part of the company of guests. This happens after the people initially invited have spurned the king's invitation, and servants are sent out to gather others to the banquet: "So the slave returned and reported this to his master. Then the owner of the house became angry and said to his slave, 'Go out at once into the streets and lanes of the town and bring in the poor, the crippled, the blind, and the lame'" (Luke 14:21).

While much more analysis and discussion are required to thoroughly explain these texts, the Jesus of the Gospels presents this vision of the Kingdom in response to the abuses of Roman imperial power and his ideal for the restoration of the people of Israel and the establishment of a just society.

Conclusion

Politicians engaged in policy debates want sound bites to support their positions when talking to the media. Sometimes they will turn to a verse or phrase from the Bible because they seem ready-made for such a moment. Accompanying the citation, they believe, comes other-worldly authority that makes them correct.

However, as we have seen in this examination of work, poverty, and welfare, the texts that these politicians quote come from settings much more complex than they imagine, and more complex than their sound bite can manage. Discussions about these biblical passages call for explanation and nuance, the enemy of political debates and campaigns. The notion that a person can quote a verse and think that he or she has summarized the whole Bible's position on a particular issue is quite naïve. The Bible often contains competing visions or analyses of situations, and it can sometimes even disagree with itself. One has to wonder if a meeting between an author in the tradition of Proverbs and the prophet Amos might result in a huge argument about what causes poverty and how Israel should address it. Further, while some texts seem to offer grace and concern toward the poor, this may come up short by some modern standards. For example, the Torah directs Israel to leave the edges of the field unharvested and not to pass through a field a second time. This portion is for the poor. However, such policies may still display an inadequate sensitivity to the struggles of poor people. For example, we do not know what would happen to the elderly or the disabled who could not gather food. Also, the policy may even be an attempt to handle and manage the poor.

Finally, the social and economic differences between the ancient and modern worlds are great. I again emphasize that ancient Israelite society centered on agriculture, and almost all of that was local. The authors of the Bible would not know about problems that occur in modern life: global markets threatening jobs; cheaper labor in a third-world country, resulting in factory closures in a U.S. city; factory automation, eliminating the need for human employees; and unemployment in an urban setting with 60,000 people competing for a limited number of jobs. These problems are not answered by scripture sound bites, but by careful analyses, nuanced arguments, and the construction of wise, just policy.

Works Cited

Bennett, Harold V. *Injustice Made Legal: Deuteronomic Law and the Flight of Widows, Strangers, and Orphans in Ancient Israel*. Grand Rapids: Eerdmans, 2002.

Doerer, Kristen. "Rev. Jim Wallis: Who's the Radical, Jesus or the Pope?" Transcribed from PBS News Hour. *Sojourners*. https://sojo.net/about-us/news/rev-jim-wallis-who-s-radical-jesus-or-pope (accessed March 25, 2016).

Ehrman, Bart D. *The New Testament: A Historical Introduction to the Early Christian Writings*, 6th edn. Oxford: Oxford University Press, 2015.

Harrington, Daniel J. *The Gospel of Matthew*. Collegeville, MN: Liturgical Press, 1991.

Hoppe, Leslie J. "Poor." *The New Interpreter's Dictionary of the Bible*. Vol. 4, 563–564. Nashville: Abingdon, 2009.

Horsley, Richard. *Jesus and the Spiral of Violence: Popular Jewish Resistance in Roman Palestine*. Minneapolis: Fortress, 1993.

Nixon, Ron. "House Agriculture Committee Approves Farm Bill." The Caucus: The Politics and Government of the *New York Times*. May 16, 2013. http://thecaucus.blogs.nytimes.com/2013/05/16/house-agriculture-committee-approves-farm-bill/?_r=0 (accessed March 25, 2016).

RWW News. "John Hagee: 'Nasty' Welfare Recipients Don't Deserve to Eat." August 6, 2014. https://www.youtube.com/watch?v=z0j5dpme9UA (accessed March 25, 2016).

Ungar, Rick. "GOP Congressman Stephen Fincher on a Mission from God—Starve the Poor while Personally Pocketing Millions in Farm Subsides." *Forbes Opinion*. May 22, 2013. http://www.forbes.com/sites/rickungar/2013/05/22/gop-congressman-stephen-fincher-on-a-mission-from-god-starve-the-poor-while-personally-pocketing-millions-in-farm-subsidies/#6219f8bc4a6c and http://thinkprogress.org/economy/2013/05/21/2042831/congressman-who-gets-millions-in-farm-subsidies-denounces-food-stamps-as-stealing-other-peoples-money/ (accessed March 25, 2016).

6

Culture Wars, Homosexuality, and the Bible

Jonathan L. Jackson

For those inclined to the left wing of U.S. politics, the idea that nonheterosexuals or sexual minorities should be accorded equal rights as heterosexuals is typically a matter of civil rights, human rights, and social equality. For those who are more comfortable on the right-wing end of the political spectrum, there is a general opposition to the notion that nonheterosexual persons are deserving of equal rights. Some conservatives (but not all) would prefer it not even exist, based on what they see as the correct (and often uniquely Protestant) Christian basis of this country's secular government.

Many opponents of affording equal rights to nonheterosexuals follow what they view as a literal or plain-sense reading of the Bible. In this chapter, we will also employ a plain-sense reading strategy; however, in this case, we will be attempting to look at the plain meaning in the *original* context of biblical texts. Because the Bible in its original Hebrew and Greek speaks quite explicitly about certain sex acts, the reader should be prepared that we will have to name them here specifically, if clinically. It is not a political strategy to shock; it is a strategy to uncover the plain-sense of certain verses.

People are complicated as individuals, and so are the politics that emerge as people debate an idea. So, of course, political positions on nonheterosexual rights vary and are not always what one might expect. For example, contradictions appear from the right wing in ways that seek to extend compassion, dignity, and honor to the person—even as homosexual sex acts are condemned. In a similarly contradictory position, some on the left wing of the political spectrum never wanted same-sex marriage, seeking a legal partnership that they view as better, more love based, or free from preoccupations about property and its inheritance. Nevertheless, the left-leaning emphasis on civil rights, human rights, and social equality exists in strong tension with the right-leaning position that condemns the very existence of nonheterosexuality as being improper for humans under God's laws as is supposedly found in the Bible.

The problem of homosexuality

Homosexuality is a bit of a dirty word within the nonheterosexual communities of North America. Those of us who identify as nonheterosexual are taught to remember a time when the medical community decided that same-sex desire was a disease of the body and mind, namely the 1960s. In contrast to this dirty term, to use self-identifiers such as lesbian, gay, or bisexual (LGB) implies that there is far more to who you are than just sexual desire or sex itself. This is the central assumption I want to make perfectly clear: nonheterosexual identities are much more complicated than sexual desires or sexual acts. They involve ties of support, emotional bonds, and material commitments, as we shall see below.

So why do people in the United States tend to think of LGB folk as defined by sex? Principally, this is due to earlier associations made with "homosexual" as a category, first by the church, and then by the medical community.

Scholars of LGBT (LGB and transgender) drawing upon the work of Michel Foucault (1990) argue the following: The Catholic Church had long deemed that homosexual orientation itself was not considered a sin unless acted upon. Many Protestant denominations, notably branches of evangelicalism, also took this position. Since homosexuality was equated with a sinful action, this meant that it was forgivable and redeemable, through repentance and/or confession. A sin, from this religious perspective, need not stay with the soul or the body permanently.

However, in the twentieth century the medical community began to approach homosexuality as a condition needing treatment. Up until the very early 1970s, the *Diagnostic and Statistics Manual* (DSM-II) of the American Psychological Association explicitly listed homosexuality as a disease. This diagnosis is not just about sexual acts, but rather addresses a constellation of gender formation and conformity. This includes how one was brought up in a family, as well as attractions [and practices] that were considered to be sexually deviant (e.g., Gagnon and Simon 1967). This complex identity resides in the mind, and that mind is inextricably linked to the biological body. Thus, in the biomedical community, homosexuality became not a *sin*—as many in the church viewed it—but a *diagnosis* (Foucault 1990 [1978]).

One can repent from a sinful act. But while a diagnosis may have a treatment (or so the medical community had hoped), the illness is part and parcel of the mind, body, and the very personal identity of the patient. It is something like chicken pox—once the virus is in your body, infecting your cells, it is still a part of you even after the disease is cured.

Thus, a subtle but important shift occurred in the way society viewed homosexuality, first mainly from the point of view of the church—as a sin—and second from the viewpoint of the hospital—as a diagnosis. As a result of this new categorization, Foucault claims that "the sodomite had been a temporary aberration; the homosexual was now [viewed as] a species" (Foucault 1990 [1978], 48). Foucault is right. Before the medicalization of homosexuality, there was no idea of the "homosexual" as a category of person. After the twentieth-century development that viewed homosexuality as a medical disease, the homosexual was viewed as an aberrant type of person who needs to undergo treatment to conform to what is "normal," in order to correct mind, body, and identity.

For many religious Americans, this confirmed that a homosexual was not just a person committing a sexual sin, but also a scientifically confirmed, faulty kind of person—perhaps even a socially dangerous "species." Both liberal forms of Judaism such as the Reform Movement and the more liberal strands of Protestant Christianity turned to the DSM-II for understanding homosexuality.

Today's discussion of "homosexuality" emerges out of this negative history of the term. Thus, many nonheterosexuals prefer a plethora of terms that indicate a different history. For example, biological men who desire or enact attraction to men prefer terms like gay, queer, or bi. Biological women who enact or desire attraction to women may prefer terms such as lesbian, queer, bi, or dyke—since minority groups often adopt with pride terms like "dyke" that outsiders may use to denigrate them. Some prefer no terminology at all, which indicates the cultural shift away from rooting the entirety of one's selfhood in the single facet of sexual desire.

The view from the present

We therefore see in our time, in these early years of the twenty-first century, a collection of nonheterosexual identities and an expanded possibility for different understandings of genders, modes of affection, kinds of material interdependence, and family structure. I will call this plethora of possibilities "queer." How did this new identity emerge in our time?

Many answers exist. I speak as a gay man born just *after* the psychiatric community finally rejected the idea of homosexuality as a medical disease of the mind and body, and as a person who was a child during the emergence of the human immunodeficiency virus (HIV) epidemic. From this vantage point, I argue that it was *political activism* in response to the mysterious "gay cancer" (as HIV was then known) that rooted queer identities firmly in North American politics. *The homosexual "species"*—this is Foucault's term for how medicine made the homosexual a category of diseased people that you could keep away from the healthy majority by categorizing them—*is now a distinctly political being.*

So now we come to the problem. Nonheterosexual people see themselves as defined by the ties of love and affection they share, the property they hold in common with a beloved partner, the children they raise, and the community they support. Yes, there is often sex between persons in a love-based relationship, and there is sexual desire for persons of the same biological sex. However, to say you are gay is a complex identity, which is not solely about sex.

Yet certain powerful religions have historically seen nonheterosexuals as practitioners of a sinful *sex act*, not as complex people in complex relationships, inhabiting complex identities. Then, science saw them as diseased persons because of same-sex attraction. Now, LGBT folks are the subject of political debate that too often sees them once again as reduced to a sex act, not as whole people.

And yes, the Bible does address a sex act and not a kind of person or a kind of love, as we're about to see.

Hebrew Bible: Sex acts, silences, and glancing affirmations

When we hold a notion, a word, or a concept in our hands at the present time and when we know that this notion, word, or concept has a particular history, we tend to think that history led directly and clearly to the present moment. We forget as we look down into the well of the past from the high surface of the present that many strands of history from the ancient past never made it to us. We often forget that how we read a term today does not necessarily reflect the original, intended meaning of the first few to write it down. Thus, when a speaker might say to a queer-identifying person that they support "homosexual rights," the intended beneficiary of such a statement might cringe at having been labeled with a term that in past decades medical terminology had equated with a disease.

Likewise, the scriptural traditions of Judaism and Christianity contain words with meanings that resonate differently depending on the cultural moment in which they were written or read. We read things one way, but the original or nearly original audience might have had many other meanings evident to them. Often cited in anti-queer arguments is the following verse from Leviticus: "Do not lie with a male as one lies with a woman; it is an abhorrence" (Lev. 18:22, JPS). This seems to be, in plain-sense modern reading, a direct ban against homosexuality.

However, turning to the plain-sense original meaning, the verse does not address contemporary issues such as same-sex relationships or marriage. It deals with the practice of some sex act. Thus, when interpreting Leviticus 18:22 to ascertain the Bible's position on "homosexuality" or queerness, three questions arise.

First, what *exactly* is the practice specified and prohibited?

The meaning of the Hebrew differs from what is captured in the English translation. The words "lie with a male as one lies with a woman" in Hebrew are more literally rendered "and with a man, not should you lie the *lyings of a woman*" (Lev. 18:22). What is immediately evident from this more literal rendering of the Hebrew text is that there is one sex practice that is forbidden here: the "lyings of a woman" (*miškevey 'išah*). What on earth are the lyings of a woman?

In fact, the Hebrew terms used are extremely explicit, but their meaning does not always translate well into English. Simply put, the Bible forbids anal sex. Grammatically speaking, the word "lyings" is a verb form in biblical Hebrew that comes from the root š-k-b, meaning "to lie down." Hebrew dictionaries explain that this phrase implies lying down in preparation for sexual intercourse (Brown, Driver, and Briggs 1999 [1906], 1012 col. 1). In the present context of Leviticus 18:22, then, the meaning is distinctly "sodomy," male–male anal sex (Brown et al. 1999). The reader should note first that this verse bans a singular, specific sex act; it does not ban sex between two men wholesale, since this practice is only one of many things two male bodies could do together. Being gay, lesbian, or bi is about so much more than a single sex act.

Second, now that we understand what sex act is specified, does the verse speak to a ban on all identities of queerness as they are understood within our present cultural context?

Clearly, the answer is no. First, thinking of male–male sex only in terms of this prohibited sexual act assumes sex is penetrative, which today not all sexual practices are. Further, to apply this sex act as constituting queerness or homosexuality itself ignores the social, emotional, material, and affective aspects of nonheterosexuality, and other such important, relational dimensions of the present-time identity. Not all queer folk or homosexuals are male-bodied individuals engaging in relations(hips) with other male-bodied individuals. The ban on a man penetrating another man therefore does not apply to lesbians, transgender persons, and so on.

At the most, Leviticus 18:22 is a ban on insertive anal sex. What is interesting upon a close reading is that the ban is only for one of the two partners involved. Oddly, the passage makes no mention of the individual being penetrated. The sex act is imagined to have one active participant, the other being "just there" as we might say. This brings up another assumption in the text that we may find uncomfortable when it is applied uncritically to the present day. It assumes that female-bodied persons have no agency in sexual intercourse.

In the vocabulary of the queer community, especially that subset identifying as "gay," penetrative anal sex practice includes two active roles. There is the role of "top," the insertive partner, and the role of "bottom," the receiving partner. Thus, the Bible here comments not on an identity as we understand queerness or homosexuality, but rather on a single-sex practice, and not even as that particular practice is understood in the queer community—as having two active participants.

It is interesting to note how some gay-identifying Orthodox Jews understand this passage. They strive to observe the law technically and correctly. Thus, they take seriously this ban and do not engage in anal sex, but continue to be "gay," sometimes in same-sex love relationships. Leviticus makes no claim on nonheterosexuality.

Thus, given the specific ancient context of Leviticus and the ways in which it differs from our modern context, the final question that arises is: Can we so simply apply the meaning of this verse to today, to our contemporary political debates?

The bedroom in the courtroom

In U.S. politics, the practice of penetrative anal sex has come before the Supreme Court recently in the case of *Lawrence et al. v. Texas* 539 U.S. 6 (2003), which overturned the 1974 Texas Sexual Conduct Law (Jakobsen and Pellegrini 2004). The issue of "sodomy" came before the high court years earlier in the case of *Bowers v. Hardwick* 487 U.S. 196 (1986), which ruled that the Georgia sodomy law as governing a private act in a private bedroom was legal and within the bounds of the constitution. As Jakobsen and Pellegrini note: "In justifying the decision, the *Bowers* majority cited millennia of moral opposition to homosexual sodomy. On closer examination, though, this supposedly universal opposition turned out to be religious in origin—what Chief Justice Warren Burger, in his concurring opinion, even explicitly named as

'Judaeo[*sic*]-Christian moral and ethical standards'" (Jakobsen and Pellegrini 2004, x, citing *Bowers v. Hardwick* 487 U.S. 196 [1986]).

Yet *Bowers* is overturned in *Lawrence v. Texas*, as explained in the majority decision by Associate Justice Anthony Kennedy:

> To say that the issue in *Bowers* was simply the right to engage in certain sexual conduct demeans the claim the individual put forward, just as it would demean a married couple were it to be said that marriage is simply about the right to have sexual intercourse. The laws involved in *Bowers* and here ... have more-far-reaching consequences, touching upon the most private human conduct, sexual behavior, and in the most private of places, the home. (Jakobsen and Pellegrini 2004, xi, citing *Lawrence et al. v. Texas* 539 U.S. 6 [2003])

We note in Justice Kennedy's language the idea that *a sex act does not constitute an entire constellation of personhood*, an entire identity when he uses the logic of analogy to say that "marriage is not simply about the right to have sexual intercourse" (Jakobsen and Pellegrini 2004).

What, then, does the Bible have to say of a fuller, more complex nonheterosexual relationship?

A story of relationships, not sex

1 Samuel 18:1–6 (JPS trans.) reads as follows:

> When [David] finished speaking with Saul, Jonathan's soul became bound up with the soul of David; Jonathan loved David as himself. Saul took him [into his service] that day and would not let him return to his father's house. Jonathan and David made a pact, because [Jonathan] loved him as himself. Jonathan took off the cloak and tunic he was wearing and gave them to David, together with his sword, bow, and belt. ...

Girded with the material support from the king's son's gear, David is successful in battle. As a result of his victory, he marries the king's daughter Michal and David grows in the eyes of the public, which regards him as a great warrior: "And they cherished his name greatly" (1 Sam. 18:30).

The affective bond between two men also helped undergird a Davidic dynasty sacred to God in the Bible, one essential to later emergent Judaism, and one that has messianic outcomes for later Christians. The intimacy between the men is remarkable. As the text states: "the soul of Jonathan became bound up with the soul of David... Jonathan, out of his love for David, adjured him again, for he loved him as himself" (1 Sam. 18:1; 20:17).

To be clear, I am not stating David and Jonathan's relationship necessarily implies a gay attraction and bonding, although some commentators on the passage have concluded this to be the case. In fact, many practicing Jews and believing Christians see this as a biblically approved model for loving relations between two people of the same sex. Jonathan and David's love is made material not in *miškevey 'išah*, the penetrative sex forbidden in Leviticus 18:22, but in the weaponry that preserves the future king's life, ensuring his accession of the throne of Judah. It is also made real by an unbreakable emotional bond.

New Testament terms and their context: Natural tops and natural bottoms

Turning again not to complex relationships, but rather to simple sex practices, we ask: But what of female-bodied persons (who, so far, seem to just lie there both as the object of Levitical laws and passive recipients of sex)?

In the letter to the Romans 1:26–27, Paul writes: "For this reason God gave them up to degrading passions. Their women exchanged natural intercourse for unnatural, and in the same way also the men, giving up natural intercourse with women, were consumed with passion for one another. Men committed shameless acts with men and received in their own persons due penalty for this error" (trans. Brooten 1996, 215). As moderns and as North Americans, it is all too tempting to read quickly the terms natural and unnatural under the dominant rubric of our biomedical sciences, which taught us for decades that "natural" is heterosexual and "unnatural" is nonheterosexual, even though this disease model was finally removed from the DSM in 1973.

How do we think about nature? We consider nature to be as survival of the fittest, according to the influence of Charles Darwin and Alfred Wallace (the codiscoverers of evolution theory). What do the fittest do when they survive? They reproduce more of themselves. We might be tempted to see nature in the New Testament as affirming this logic. But this logic of survival and reproduction is new and of our time. In Paul's day, the natural intercourse that he meant to imply was what the Roman Empire thought of as proper sex—passive women lying under active men.

Brooten offers a corrective by explaining what "nature" meant when Paul was composing his letters to the early Christian communities. By keying in on these terms "natural" and "unnatural," she argues that: "… Paul condemns sexual relations between women as 'unnatural' because he shares the widely held [Hellenistic] cultural view that *women are passive by nature* and therefore should remain passive in sexual relations" (Brooten 1996, 216). She argues that women, according to this ancient thinking, "cannot naturally assume the active role [as opposed to the passive], thus rendering natural sexual relations between women impossible" (Brooten 1996). By this logic, those who now call themselves lesbian could not have *existed* in the logic of Roman sexuality.

Brooten further explains that in bringing early Christianity to the non-Jewish world at large, Paul is trying to match up the Jewish idea of natural sexual relations with the Roman. The Jewish law forbids male–male anal sex in Leviticus as explained above. Good Roman thinking sees passive women and active men in sex. Following Brooten's commentary, any sexual role in which the woman does not lie as the passively inserted partner during sex is condemned.

Once again, understanding that sex is not the most important or the complete part of gay, lesbian, or bi identity reveals that not only does this passage fail to address our contemporary ideas of LGBT as a complex way to be a person in this society, it also does not address our understanding of what is natural and what is not natural. The Bible therefore does not address either female–female or male–male homosexuality as a complex construct of who one is; rather, it bans certain sex acts in a very specific and explicit manner.

Later on in her argument, Brooten further observes that two other supposed references to what we once called homosexual and now call LGBT sexuality are found in 1 Corinthians 6:9 and 1 Timothy 1:10, which read as follows. The 1 Corinthians letter addresses male–male anal penetration, forbidding a single sex act already outlawed in Leviticus, with the Greek literally speaking of "one who has sex with a man as sex with a woman." This indicates Paul's concern is not with a type of person or a whole identity, but with a sex act already forbidden in the Levitical code, as inherited from his Jewish upbringing and first career. The same analysis applies to the 1 Timothy reference—it is a reaffirmation of the Leviticus ban on a single sex act.

Our notions today of being gay, lesbian, and bisexual are so much broader than the ancient worlds of the Bible could conceive. They encompass relationships and identities far more complex than a single sex act. They are not in today's present time a reincarnation of ancient Roman, Hellenistic, or biblical Israelite sexuality. As Justice Kennedy observes: "To say that the issue in *Bowers* was simply the right to engage in certain sexual conduct demeans the claim the individual put forward, just as it would demean a married couple were it to be said that marriage is simply about the right to have sexual intercourse. The laws involved in *Bowers* and here…have more-far-reaching consequences, touching upon the most private human conduct, sexual behavior, and in the most private of places, the home" (Jakobsen and Pellegrini 2004, xi, citing *Lawrence et al. v. Texas* 539 U.S. 6 [2003]).

Interpreting the past in present: An identity is so much more than sex

Standing at the present time, looking down into the well of the past, we can see there are ideals that exist now that did not exist in the past, and vice versa. The idea that a relationship between two persons (whether heterosexual or nonheterosexual) is not reducible to a form of sexual intercourse is key to the North American understanding of sexual identity. The early church or the editors, compilers, and writers of the Hebrew Bible could not have imagined or understood nonheterosexual relationships from this perspective.

In her foundational article, *Thinking Sex*, anthropologist Gayle Rubin writes:

> The time has come to think about sex…people are likely to become dangerously crazy about sexuality. Contemporary

conflicts over sexual values and erotic conduct have much in common with the religious disputes of earlier centuries. They acquire immense symbolic weight. Disputes over sexual behavior often become the vehicles for displacing social anxieties, and discharging their attendant emotional intensity. Consequently, sexuality should be treated with special respect in times of great stress. (Rubin in Abelove, Barale, and Halperin 1993, 3–4)

While I share her concern, we have to be careful now, in the second decade of the twenty-first century, not to conflate a sex practice with a sexuality. We see this anxiety in Brooten, who shows us how Paul attempts to align Jewish and Roman social orders in his condemnation of sexual practices. The practices that Paul condemns ignore both the "natural" active and penetrating role of men, and also ignore the "natural" passive and penetrated role of women.

But *against* the sex-centered language that Rubin (1993) deploys, we need to look *away* from sex sometimes to see the whole person named by the singular facet of sexual desire. Paul does not condemn those whom we now call lesbians, since such an identity did not exist in his day. Such an identity as "lesbian" is dependent on modern and contemporary feminist and women's liberation movements, on political coalition with HIV activists, with the complexities of affective (love, mutuality, and intimacy) and material (property, privacy of domicile, and inheritance jurisprudence) sharing. We see the biblical compilers and editors praise such relationships, as typified in examples such as the affective love and material sharing of the tools of warriorship between Jonathan and David, just as we see today the Supreme Court affirm the relationship between same-sex persons in cases such as the recent landmark *Obergefell et al. v. Hodges 567* U.S. (2015):

This dynamic can be seen in the Nation's experience with gay and lesbian rights. Well into the 20th century, many States condemned same-sex intimacy as immoral, and homosexuality was treated as an illness. Later in the century, cultural and political developments allowed same-sex couples to lead more open and public lives. Extensive public and private dialogue followed, along with shifts in public attitudes. (*Obergefell et al. v. Hodges 567* U.S. [2015])

It is the dignity of persons in material, deeply emotional, and enduring relationships—regardless of the biomedical sex of their bodies—whom the high court has seen fit to honor with equal social position. The sex act is not the relationship, nor does it constitute the entirety of persons who are sexual minorities. This was not true in the time of the composition and editing of the Bible, and it is not true today at a time when the Bible is inherited and consumed politically.

Works Cited

Brooten, B.J. *Love between Women: Early Christian Responses to Female Homoeroticism*. Chicago, IL: University of Chicago Press, 1996.

Brown, F. Driver, S. and Briggs, C. *The Brown-Driver-Briggs Hebrew and English Lexicon: With an Appendix Containing the Biblical Aramaic*. Peabody, MA: Hendrickson Publishers, 1999.

Danker, F.W. (ed.). *A Greek-English Lexicon of the New Testament and Other Early Christian Literature*, 3rd edn. Chicago, IL: University of Chicago Press, 2000 [1957].

Foucault, M. *The History of Sexuality. Vol. 1: An Introduction*, trans. Robert Hurley. New York: Vintage Books, 1990 [1978].

Gagnon, J.H. and Simon, W. *Sexual Deviance*. New York: Harper and Row, 1967.

Jakobsen, J. and Pellegrini, A. *Love the Sin: Sexual Regulation and the Limits of Religious Tolerance*. Boston, MA: Beacon Press, 2004.

Rubin, Gayle. "Thinking Sex" In *The Lesbian and Gay Studies Reader*, edited by H. Abelove, M.A. Barale and D. Halperin. New York: Routledge Press, 1993.

7

The Bible and the Divine Sanctioning of Governments

Colleen Shantz

Anyone who has read through the chapters to this point in the book will by now have a solid sense of how the Bible is sometimes misused in political debate. They will also likely have a sense of many points of potential disagreement with public policies or discomfort with the biblical teaching—or both. But one hardly needs additional education on the possibility of political disagreement. Its signs are everywhere of late. A case in point: on the evening of March 2, 2016, otherwise known as Super Tuesday, Google searches for "how can I move to Canada" spiked 350 percent. Simon Rogers, a data editor for Google, tweeted out the news (@smfrogers). In light of such enthusiasm, it could be a good time for a little sober reflection on some of the differences between the two countries.

Consider this: among the best-known phrases from U.S. founding documents are the rights to "bear arms" and to "life, liberty, and the pursuit of happiness." By contrast, for its constitution, Canada adopted the Commonwealth emphasis on "peace, order, and good government" as the primary purpose of parliamentary power. Where the United States secured its independence through acts of civil disobedience—like dumping taxed tea into the Boston harbor—and revolution, Canada slowly negotiated its way to a de facto independence, with its own Charter of Rights and Freedoms, but still legally under the rule of Queen Elizabeth and her heirs.

Both countries have their share of political discontent with peaceful public demonstrations against police violence, tuition fees, corporate scandals, and public policy on the streets of major cities on both sides of our shared border. And we are not alone. Indeed, signs of discontent in our two countries, western Europe, and Japan have been around at least since the 1970s when an international study reported that "Dissatisfaction with, and lack of confidence in, the functioning of the institutions of democratic government have thus now become widespread" (Crozier et al. 1975). The 1980s and 1990s only increased the trend of dissatisfaction (Newton and Norris 1999). But given this shared unease, it's worth noting that some kinds of protest are distinctive to the American context. Take, for instance, the armed occupation of a government facility by the Oregon militia because of their rejection of the right of the U.S. government to own land.

A similar case can be made for the circumstances surrounding Kim Davis, the county clerk who refused to issue a marriage license because of her disagreement with a legal ruling. Davis claimed that natural law superseded civic law and was eventually charged with contempt of court after refusing to comply with two court orders to fulfill this part of her job. Rather than resign, Davis claimed religious freedom. The distinctive American character of these events is not so much in Davis's objection but in the way her actions were celebrated in political circles. Indeed, during the 2016 presidential primaries, two candidates—Mike Huckabee and Ted Cruz—actually traveled to Grayson, Kentucky, to stand at Davis's side during a press conference held to cover her release from jail. In fact, an aide to Huckabee made it clear that the press conference was in fact a campaign event: "We planned, paid for, and promoted the event and Sen. Cruz showed up the day of and tried to take it over. It would have been the equivalent to us showing up at their religious liberty event in Iowa a couple weeks ago, claiming it was our event, and expecting to give the keynote speaking role... First time any of us have ever seen a presidential candidate crash another candidate's event without so much as reaching out to get permission to attend. Bizarre" (*Politico*, September 9, 2015).

Despite this focus on Chistianity, despite the fact that at that news conference candidate Huckabee repeated his sense that God

was acting throughout American history, he did not quote the
Bible. Instead he claimed revelation in history: "I do not think it is
possible to explain America apart from the providence of almighty
God. There is no other explanation for how this country came into
being." He flirted with the idea that Davis was a new incarnation:
"God showed up ... in the form of an elected Democrat named Kim
Davis." He even quoted *Forrest Gump*, but not the Bible.

The Bible would not have helped Huckabee's particular case.
In Romans 13, it speaks pretty directly to circumstances like those
of Davis and the impromptu militia in Oregon: "Let every person
subject her or himself to the governing authorities. For there is
no authority except by God and whatever authorities exist have
been appointed by God. So the one who resists the authority has
opposed what God has appointed" (Rom. 13:1–2; translated by
Jewett 2007). Given that clear claim, it's interesting that politicians
do not quote the Bible in these situations. For the most part, other
cases in this volume consider the ways politicians have used the
Bible to address various policy issues. But in this case, as far as
I know, no contemporary politician has used Romans 13:1–8
(or 1 Pet. 2:11–17) to justify her or his position. Instead, typically
the passage is quoted by the supporters of various politicians in
order to silence opposition. The comments sections of various
campaign websites are sprinkled with such references.

This reluctance was not always the case. For example, James I,
King of England from 1603 to 1625, and the patron behind the King
James Version of the Bible vigorously supported "the divine right of
kings." He cited the Psalms as evidence, because, he claimed, they
describe kings as gods. Furthermore, in a clear reference to Romans
13 he described kings as "God's lieutenants." Two centuries before
James I, Dante imagined the ninth and deepest circle of hell to be
reserved for traitors (*Inferno*). There, he pictured Judas clasped in
Satan's jaws, but right alongside were Brutus and Cassius, who
betrayed Julius Caesar. It seems remarkable that Dante would
count these betrayals as equal, but it is not out of keeping with
interpretations of Romans 13.

Before moving to a discussion of the passage in Romans 13,
consider one more example of a group who took it to heart.
In this case, the thoughts come from one of the Russian Orthodox
nuns who were murdered by the secret police in the late 1930s.
The transcript from her interrogation shows that she had Romans

13 in mind as she faced the authorities and was eventually martyred.
Here is the record of their conversation:

>—What are your convictions and views about the Soviet
>government?
>—As a believer, I understand every government to be from God,
>and it does not concern me who has power at the present moment
>in the Soviet Union.
>—As a monastic have you been subject to repression from the
>side of the Soviet government?
>—As a monastic I have been deprived of a right to vote.
>—You were arrested for counter-revolutionary activities that
>you undertook with other nuns of the Novodevichii Monastery.
>The interrogation requires a truthful response.
>—I went into an apartment with the nuns Evdokia
>(Golovanova) and Matrona (Lipatova). I said that a difficult
>time has arrived … [and] believers are discontent with the Soviet
>government … The Soviet government is robbing monasteries
>[and] closing churches, but soon they will pay with their lives
>[and] everyone will then know that there is a God.[1]

Clearly, there are diverse responses to Romans 13, all from
people who claimed Christian identity. Does the passage give us
any help in sorting them out?

Three issues in the interpretation
of Romans 13

While most people listen for meaning in the Bible as
straightforwardly as they might read a blog post, biblical scholars
read with particular attention to differences in social and cultural
setting. This attention shouldn't come as a surprise because we
all know that there are plenty of circumstances where the context
makes all the difference in communication. Think of two people
telling you they "missed you": one of them emerging from a
recently landed airline flight and the other holding a carton of
eleven (and only eleven) eggs. One of the difficulties of listening
for meaning in the Bible, especially in Paul's letters to the churches,

is that we have only half of a conversation, a little like overhearing someone talking on a cell phone. As a result, listeners often create a picture of the context and the conversation partner based on less than half the evidence.

In the case of these two passages, there are three kinds of differences that are especially relevant to the communication: (1) the same word can denote different things—even a word like taxes, (2) the historical political situation shapes both the writers and the audience, and (3) the form of communication tells us something about meaning. The next three sections address these issues in turn.

Taxes by any other name

The practice of collecting taxes is nearly as old as it is inevitable. Paul and the members of the Roman assembly faced their own tax bills:

> For the same reason you also pay tribute, for the authorities are God's servants, busy with this very thing. Pay to all what is due them—tribute to whom tribute are due, taxes to whom taxes is due, respect to whom respect is due, honor to whom honor is due. (Romans 13:6–7; author's translation)

But this passage lists a couple of different forms of tax, mixed in with other kinds of civic obligations. Verse 6 reminds the Roman congregation that they already pay the tribute tax in order both to avoid punishment and to appease their own consciences. Verse 7 adds to this an import tax, which applied to trade in goods. This may sound like a personal tax and a sales tax—not unlike the situation most of us find ourselves in.

However, there are a few significant differences between those taxes and ours. First, the case of the tribute (or *phronos*, in Greek) is a kind of head tax that was collected from citizens in regions that Rome had colonized. So, for example, the people of ancient Palestine paid a tribute tax to Rome after Rome conquered their lands. They didn't benefit from the tribute money, which was spent hundreds of miles away. It was a classic case of taxation without representation. In addition, a flat price per person, regardless of resources, is the most regressive form of taxation.

Normally, Roman citizens were exempt from paying the tribute. They got to benefit from some of that cash flowing in, but did not have to contribute. However, the case for immigrants who had moved to the city from conquered provinces was different. They were treated as if they still lived outside of Rome. Unlike their next-door neighbors who were citizens, these residents of Rome were required to pay the tribute despite living within the city's bounds (Coleman 1997). Paul's wording in verse 6 makes it clear that the congregation in Rome mostly, if not wholly, belongs to this tribute-paying category. They are subject people living in the territory of their victors and they paid the price. Is "tax" the right word for this payment? It's more like a penalty creating two categories of residents.

The second word Paul uses (*telos*, in Greek) indicates a tax on goods and services—everything from pomegranates to prostitution. There was also a kind of licensing fee for those who worked in various trades. You paid a *telos* to be allowed to fish for a living or to weave. While this form of tax may seem more just—after all, the people who paid it were at least able to buy things and to work for a living—there were problems with the way it was administered. More on that in a minute, but meanwhile, the takeaway point is that these "taxes" did not much resemble our taxes. Where ours help to provide public education, libraries, and unemployment insurance, theirs were extractive and unregulated. Yet Paul urges people to pay them anyway and, furthermore, to respect and honor the authorities while they were doing it.

The political context in the letter to the Romans

We know a surprising amount about the city of Rome in the first century, when Paul wrote his letter to the Romans. Part of that information comes from a first-century senator and historian named Tacitus. One of the most interesting sets of events that Tacitus records occurs in 58 C.E. Now most people think that the letter to the Romans was written sometime between 55 and 58, just before these events. You won't be surprised to hear that part of the report from Tacitus concerned taxes.

I mentioned that there were problems with the indirect taxes (licensing fees and sales taxes) and this concerned the way they were collected. In Book 13 of his *Annals*, Tacitus reports that taxes were collected by revenue-farmers. Rome did not keep bureaucrats on a stable salary in order to administer taxes; instead the right to collect such revenue was sold at auction to the highest bidder. In turn these tax-farmers had to make their profits by adding a percentage to the amount of tax that was due. The opportunity for abuse is obvious and was frequently pursued. The local population began to complain and resist the taxation. The situation in Rome became volatile in the mid- to late 50s and was so tense by 58 C.E. that Nero considered doing away with all the indirect taxes just to appease the public and avoid riots. However, he was prevented from doing so by his advisors. Here's how Tacitus described it:

> Nero hesitated whether he ought not to decree the abolition of all indirect taxation and present the reform as the noblest of gifts to the human race. His impulse, however, was checked by his older advisers, who pointed out that the dissolution of the empire was certain if the revenues on which the state subsisted were to be curtailed: "For, the moment the duties on imports were removed, the logical sequel would be a demand for the abrogation of the direct taxes." (Tacitus, *Annals* 13.50)

In other words, they saw a slippery slope ahead. If you get rid of the taxes, the next thing you know, people will want to get rid of the tribute as well—and that would require restraint on the part of the elite. In the end, the taxes remained, but more controls were placed on the margins of the tax collectors.

Paul wrote to Rome as these tensions were mounting, before the official protest in 58 C.E. His concern was specific, not general. He was not writing with an overarching political theory in mind. Rather, he was writing with a sense of the trouble that could arise in a city like Rome if private grumbling broke out into public retribution. His advice was to pay the tribute and the taxes—even though they were unjust. Furthermore, he urged respect and honor for those who collected the fees because in Paul's mind none of this mattered very much. To Paul's mind something much greater than taxes was afoot.

The medium is (part of) the message

The third difference in communication that I mentioned earlier has to do with the form. Romans 13 is part of a section of short bits of wisdom strung together into a block of advice sometimes called paraenesis. The teachings that are collected in such sections are often traditional rather than specially created for the occasion. Sometimes when you read them it can feel like there is no order in these strings and no significant relationship among the sayings. However, in Romans 12–13 we can see some signs that Paul was framing the section.

Paul includes "paraenesis" near the end of most of his letters—sections that counsel, exhort, or give advice. And I empathize with his choice. I often communicate like this at the end of a phone conversation with my son who is away at university: remember that sometimes it helps to freewrite without editing your essays as you go; don't forget that food fuels your brain too; make sure you get enough sleep. It's advice that is always true, but I tailor it to be especially relevant for the point in the school term when we are communicating. My son knows how to hear it. And if I'm careful not to give too long a string of motherly wisdom, among the things he hears are my care and love for him.

So too with Paul, often there is nothing particularly special in his counsel except for its timeliness and the care that is expressed through it. Even the advice about submitting to governments—despite its relevance to the tax situation—is not original to Romans. Lots of people in the first century thought this way. Seneca, a Stoic philosopher, and Philo, a Jewish one, both agreed that to respect of those of higher rank was to respect God. And earlier Israelite tradition includes both a critique of kings and a sense that God works through even the most abusive rulers. For example, the prophet Jeremiah repeatedly claims that the Babylonian King Nebuchadnezzar is God's servant in punishing Israel (see Jer. 21:7; 21:10; 22:25; 25:9; 27:6–9; 32:28; 43:10; 46:13; 49:30–33; compare Ezek. 26:7–12 with Dan. 1:1–2).

However, as I mentioned, sometimes in paraenesis the arrangement of the sayings tells us something about the overall meaning and that is the case in Romans. Two features are especially important: (1) the opening and closing frame of the section and (2) its climax in the obligation to love (Rom. 13:8–10).

Here's how the passage begins:

I appeal to you therefore,…to present your bodies as a living sacrifice, holy and acceptable to God, which is your spiritual worship. Do not be conformed to the pattern of this world but be transformed by the renewing of your minds, so that you may discern what is the will of God—what is good and acceptable and perfect. (Rom. 12:1–2)[2]

It's an invitation to think outside of the box, even if they are using traditional teachings to do so. The section of paraenesis ends by reminding the Roman audience that the time is short and "the day is near" (Rom. 13:11–12). That is a clear reference to Paul's understanding that the world as they knew it would soon come to an end. This framing suggests that whatever people do, they should do it with recognition that things are changing and current priorities are false.

The Russian nun that I quoted in the opening section had this view. The monasteries were being plundered and religious people were being executed but soon the perpetrators "will pay with their lives [and] everyone will then know that there is a God." It is a view that produces quietism in the face of political abuse. There is no need to work for change because soon business as usual will be over anyway. Paul was certainly wrong about the shortness of the time. Quietism seems less palatable as the time stretches on.

But rejection of quietism does not mean there are no options but the Oregon militia. Paul is not merely quietistic in this section. He does not only say, stick to the status quo, and give people what they expect from you (Rom. 13:7). Immediately after the advice on governments, he brings the section to a crescendo with some wisdom that qualifies all of his sayings: "[O]we no one anything, except to love one another; for the one who loves another has fulfilled the law.…Love does no wrong to a neighbor; therefore, love is the fulfilling of the law" (Rom. 13:8, 10). In the structure of this section, the short section on love provides the key for interpreting all the rest, including one's relationship to government. In Paul's political triage, love is the highest law of all. Whatever else people do should fulfill the obligation to love.

The wisdom of love

I found it surprisingly difficult to get started on this chapter, partly because the topic does not seem to have the kind of urgency of something like climate change or the controversy of the host of public issues related to sexuality. There is no exciting conclusion to draw from a passage like Romans 13:1–8. It is a passage that invites slow, careful discernment, not fire-in-the-belly social change.

For people who would point to Christian misuse of their own scripture there is little to work with in this case. Politicians tend to avoid this passage (thankfully) and citizens tend to use it only to shut down opposition to their favored candidates or issues. In short, it rarely receives blanket application by anyone. For those who try to shape their lives by the Bible, this passage seems impossible to apply without qualification. Since the *Shoah*—the systematic slaughter during World War II of people because of particular religious and/or ethnic identities (especially Jews), physical and mental disabilities, or sexual orientation—it has become untenable to imagine that God authorizes all states. Indeed, this lesson has been forgotten and relearned at various points in history. Would Paul himself have written in the same way that he wrote in Romans 13 if he had composed the letter later in Nero's reign? After 64 C.E. when Nero began to actively persecute Christians to take attention away from his abuses of power? Indeed, Paul often did say something different about political authorities, for example, a couple of chapters earlier when he notes that principalities and powers have no effect in matters related to God (Rom. 8:38–39).

However, Paul's tempering words about a debt of love are the bit of wisdom that does apply at all times. Furthermore, that wisdom is directly relevant to political engagement. The same theorists that I quoted in the introduction to this essay also reflected on the remedy to the political malaise that they studied. Here's what they wrote:

> Social trust can help build effective social and political institutions, which can help governments perform effectively, and this in turn encourages confidence in civic institutions. Thus, Trilateral nations that enjoy a high level of social trust also tend to enjoy a relatively high level of confidence in political institutions. Conversely, countries with low levels of social trust

are less likely to build the kind of vibrant civil society that spurs strong government performance, and the result will be low citizen confidence in government and public institutions. (Newton and Norris 1999, 12)

They go on to say that the effect no doubt runs the other way as well: corrupt or ineffectual governments erode social trust, generating a cycle that exacerbates the problem. "Owe no one anything except to love one another" begins to sound like good political advice. By observing laws whenever possible we make trust feasible. Laws provide a shared network of expectation that facilitates democratic change.

But still, such observations do not make for exciting political conventions. Any application of Romans 13 requires the kind of prolonged and thoughtful negotiation of meaning that does not meet the character limit of a tweet or the plot twists of reality TV. Nor is it amenable to unleashing the surge of emotion that can fuel a change of heart. But that is often the way of wisdom. It's complicated. Its force is slow and quiet. It depends on more than one thing and distinctions among the situations in which it must be applied.

Actually, it requires something a lot like the careful discernment of Martin Luther King Jr. in his interview on *Meet the Press* in 1965:

I think we all have moral obligations to obey just laws. On the other hand I think we have moral obligations to disobey unjust laws because noncooperation with evil is as much a moral obligation as is cooperation with good. I think the distinction here is that when one breaks a law that conscience tells him is unjust he must do it openly, he must do it cheerfully, he must do it lovingly, he must do it civilly, not uncivilly, and he must do it with a willingness to accept the penalty and anyone who breaks a law that conscience tells him is unjust, and willingly accepts the penalty by staying in jail in order to arouse the conscience of the community on the injustice of the law, is at that moment expressing the very highest respect for the law. (King 1965)

In his earlier interview on *Meet the Press* (1960), he added that those who are willing to break unjust laws and take the punishment determined by authorities for doing so "are those who are part of the saving of the nation." That sounds a lot like respect for authorities, love of others, and service of God. If you watch that 1965 episode (it's available on YouTube), you will see that King's answers are delivered slowly and in measured tone. Perhaps that is just the right pace for wise thinking about our relationship with political powers.

Works Cited

Burgess, John. "Prepodobnomuchenitsa Mariia (Tseitlin)." In *Novomucheniki moskovskogo Novodevich'ego Monastyria: The New Martyrs of Moscow's Novodevichii Monastery*. Moscow: Novodevichii Monastery, 2006.

Burgess, John. "Religious Persecution and Religious Freedom: The Witness of Russia's New Martyrs and Holy Elders." In *Thinking across Boundaries: Interdisciplinary Approaches to Theological Inquiry*, edited by Robin W. Lovin and Joshua T. Mauldin. Eerdmans, chapter 5, in press.

Coleman, Thomas M. "Binding Obligations in Romans 13:7: A Semantic Field and Social Context." *Tyndale Bulletin* 48 (1997): 307–327.

Crozier, Michel, Huntington, Samuel P. and Watanuki, Joji. *The Crisis of Democracy*. New York: New York University Press, 1975.

"Interview with Martin Luther King Jr." *Meet the Press*. NBC, Washington, D.C. March 28, 1965. https://www.youtube.com/watch?v=fAtsAwGreyE (accessed March 23, 2016).

Jewett, Robert. *Romans: A Commentary*. Hermeneia—A Critical and Historical Commentary on the Bible. Minneapolis: Fortress Press, 2007.

Newton, Kenneth and Norris, Pippa. "Confidence in Public Institutions: Faith, Culture or Performance?" Atlanta, GA: John F. Kennedy School of Government, Harvard University, 1999. http://www.hks.harvard.edu/fs/pnorris/Acrobat/NEWTON.PDF (accessed March 29, 2016).

Strauss, Daniel. "Huckabee Complains Cruz Crashed His Party." *Politico*. September 9, 2015. http://www.politico.com/story/2015/09/mike-huckabee-kim-davis-rally-ted-cruz-213435 (accessed March 29, 2016).

Yuval-Davis, Nira. "The Double Crisis of Governability and Governmentality: Potential Political Responses to Living in a Risky Global Environment." *Soundings* 52 (2012): 88–99.

8

Teaching Evolution versus Creationism

Daniel K. Falk

"In the beginning God created the heavens and the earth," Governor Mike Huckabee responded during the third Republican Presidential debate in 2007 ("Third G.O.P. Debate," 2007). The moderator had asked, "Governor Huckabee, in a previous debate, you and two of your colleagues indicated that you do not believe in evolution…What do you believe: is it the story of creation as it is reported in the Bible?" After quoting Genesis 1:1, Huckabee continued, "To me it's pretty simple. A person either believes that God created this process, or believes that it was an accident, and that it just happened all on its own." Both the question and the answer assume an antagonistic relationship between science and faith, and reflect the gulf that divides Americans over evolution.

Since the 1925 Scopes Trial, attempts by states to prohibit the teaching of evolution in public schools have been struck down as violating the Establishment Clause in the First Amendment. In *Epperson v. Arkansas* (1968), the Supreme Court ruled that "[t]here can be no doubt that Arkansas has sought to prevent its teachers from discussing the theory of evolution because it is contrary to the belief of some that the Book of Genesis must be the exclusive source of doctrine as to the origin of man" (Masci 2014).

Subsequent state challenges sought "balanced treatment" for alternative views such as "Creation Science" or "Intelligent Design," or the requirement of disclaimers that evolution is a controversial theory. These too have been struck down as attempts to promote a particular religious viewpoint (e.g., 1987 *Edwards v. Aguillard*; 2005 *Kitzmiller v. Dover*; Boyle et al. 2005). Other bills, some of which are still pending, take a more indirect approach of appealing to academic freedom to teach "the scientific strengths or scientific weaknesses" of current scientific theories, including evolution (Lebo 2011).

Evolution explains changes in living organisms over time as a result of the survival of those genetic variations best suited to their environment and is foundational to modern biology. As a scientific theory, evolution is based on observed data and has undergone rigorous testing and confirmation. Creationism refers to views that God directly created the universe as we know it less than 10,000 years ago, usually based on a literal reading of Genesis. Creation Science seeks to reconcile scientific findings with a creationist view of human origins. Intelligent Design refrains from explicit religious language, but argues that certain "irreducibly complex" biological structures are evidence of deliberate design by an intelligent cause rather than random, natural selection (Scott 2009, 57, 105–143).

While in the political sphere promoters of creationism tend to argue that evolution is a controversial theory and should be balanced with alternative views, the internal rhetoric often presents evolution as incompatible with religious faith. For example, in a 2012 speech at Liberty Baptist Church, Rep. Paul Broun (R–GA.), a member of the House Committee on Science, Space, and Technology, called the theories of evolution and the Big Bang "lies straight from the pit of hell," and affirmed his belief that God created the world about 9,000 years ago in a literal six days (Pearce 2012). This dismissal of foundational scientific theories by a sitting member of this committee set off a firestorm in the media.

Pitting evolution against religious faith resonates with a significant demographic of the American public. According to a 2012 Gallup Poll, "46% of Americans believe in the creationist view," 32 percent believe that humans evolved with God guiding the process (theistic evolution), and only 15 percent believe that evolution alone explains the development of humans (Newport 2012). The first figure has remained virtually unchanged over eleven polls since 1982, despite enormous advances in evolutionary biology.

A 2013 survey found that 33 percent of Americans reject the theory of evolution, and that their views have strong correlation to religious and political affiliation (Pew 2013). On whether creationism or intelligent design should be taught in public schools, the American public is similarly divided: 40 percent are in favor and 32 percent are opposed (Henderson 2013). Again there is a strong correlation with political affiliation: Republicans are nearly twice as likely to favor the teaching of creationism or intelligent design in public schools as Democrats—57 percent versus 30 percent.

Teachers are on the frontlines of the struggles over evolution and creationism in public schools, caught between parents, school boards, and state standards. A series of studies by Berkman and Plutzer (2010, 2015) found that 28 percent of teachers are advocates of the theory of evolution, and 13 percent are advocates of creationism. Of the 60 percent in the "cautious middle," the vast majority accept the theory of evolution (85 percent) but ultimately undermine it in the classroom to avoid conflict or out of their own unresolved questions about the relationship between faith and evolution. One student teacher, for example, stated, "My faith is a big part of who I am and very important to me. To me, it's a question of—I believe the Bible to be true. It's a question of, in Genesis when it talks about a six day account of creation…is that a literal thing or is that a figurative literary device that's kind of poetic? I'm not really sure" (Berkman and Plutzer 2015, 11).

What does the Bible teach about creation and the origin of life? We must acknowledge that the Bible is an ancient collection of texts of various kinds, written over a long period—about a millennium—in languages and cultures very distant from our own. This collection, however, is sacred scripture for many religious communities, who hear the many voices united as one grand story. We will focus on Genesis 1–2, asking first what it means from a literary perspective, then what it means in its historical and cultural context, and finally how the Bible as a whole develops the theme of creation.

Genesis 1–2: The literary lens

At first glance, the Bible starts by telling us clearly how everything began. It situates us "in the beginning" and tells us that all things exist because God created them, speaking things into existence in a sequence of six days: light; sky and waters; land and vegetation; sun, moon, and stars; birds and fish; then animals and humans. But then in Genesis 2:4 we start all over again, and this time God doesn't speak to create, but molds humans out of clay before there were any plants or animals.

The Bible begins with *two* very different stories of origins. The first story calls God "Elohim" (translated "God"). The second story calls God "Yahweh Elohim" (translated "LORD God"). In the first story, God is distant and in serene solitude. In the second, God is intimate and anthropomorphic, a potter up to his elbows in the muck of humanity. The first is stately poetry and formulaic; the second is folksy storytelling. Various different characteristics make it clear that these are two different stories from different origins (Sarna 2001, 3–23).

When we take a closer look, we see more differences. In neither story is there any hint of creation out of nothing: in both cases, the story begins with stuff, but different stuff. In the first story, everything begins in a watery chaos, in darkness—but God is there in the breeze (Gen. 1:2). Creation is separating, sorting, and bringing order to chaos (Gen. 1:4, 6–7, 18). After putting light on the subject, God creates some room: God makes a dome to hold back the chaotic waters, forming a bubble in which to create life (Gen. 1:3, 6–7). God then restricts the waters within this biosphere so that dry land appears (Gen. 1:9). The second story, however, begins with a dry, empty desert, and God waters an oasis (Gen. 2:4–6). In the first story, humans are added at the end, on the sixth day, after everything else is in place (Gen. 1:26–28). The second story takes place in a day, and God creates humans *first*, because they are needed as gardeners to till the ground before God can plant a garden (Gen. 2:4–9). In the first story, God does not create a single man named Adam; God creates the human race that collectively— male *and* female—is called *adam* (Gen. 1:27). Then God declares it all "very good" (Gen. 1:31). In the second story, God creates humans in two stages: first an *adam* (humanoid) fashioned out of the *adamah* (earth; Gen. 2:7). This pun could be translated, "an earthling out of the earth." But it is "*not* good" because the *adam* is lonely (Gen. 2:18). In a bizarre scene that begs for imaginative reading, God parades all the animals by the human to see if one of these might be a suitable mate (Gen. 2:18–20). In the end, God fashions another being out of the first, and humanity is now female and male (Gen. 2:21–23). In the first story, there is precise order in the universe—everything has its place, and it is all "good." In the second story, God seems to be winging it, experimenting, working by trial and error.

This is not at all the same story told from two different perspectives, but two alternative stories with very different meanings. In the first story, humans are presented as the pinnacle of creation, made in "God's image," picturing humans as vice-regents of God on earth. That is, in a stunning departure from typical cultural norms in the ancient world, all humans are elevated to the place normally reserved for kings and priests. The ultimate climax is with God's cessation of creative activity on the seventh day, which God makes "holy" (Gen. 2:1–3). This story serves to promote the observance of Sabbath, a holy day central to the Israelite cultic life, which emphasizes well-being and nonexploitation. Thus, the first story ends with a utopian ideal: harmony and peace throughout creation. The second story, however, emphasizes humans as servants, and the danger in trying to rise above one's station, and it ends with the disintegration of harmony in Genesis 3. It presents the harsh realities of human existence.

That Genesis has two very different creation stories side by side without harmonizing them should signal something to the reader: these stories are not about how things came to be, but they are two different "meaning-stories." They are complementary and work together to emphasize different experiences of being in the world: the rapturous ideal of humanity elevated, which can be experienced by the community in worship (see Ps. 8); and the creatureliness of humans whose lives are brutish and short, and end in dust.

If read as literal history, these two stories would contradict each other, but that is not how they work in Genesis. They function by way of analogy, as complementary models for understanding life—somewhat like scientists explaining light as simultaneously particles and waves.

These stories do not teach the "how" of existence. Genesis 1:1–2:3 does—it must be admitted—reflect the author's understanding of the world, or cosmology. This does not, however, correspond to the actual world we know. The author of Genesis would be stunned to observe a rocket blast off and continue endlessly into space. In this ancient cosmology, the blue of the sky is a solid metal dome that holds back the primeval waters. It has doors and windows that open and shut for rain and for the sun, moon, and stars to enter and exit. The earth is a disk that floats on a great dangerous sea, held up by pillars. This view of the world is widely attested in the ancient world. Genesis 1:1–2:3 simply reflects the "science" of the day, but as we will see, this is hardly what Genesis seeks to "teach."

Genesis 1–2: The cultural lens

Around the same time that Darwin's theories were challenging literal interpretations of Genesis 1–3, cosmogonic myths (stories about the origins of the gods) from the ancient Near East were being discovered that shed new light on the Genesis creation stories. I use "myth" not in the popular usage of a false story, but in the academic sense of a symbolic story to convey ultimate truths. Myths are "meaning-stories" that go beyond raw observations. From Mesopotamia, the ancestral land of Abraham and the region in which the Israelites were in exile, came myths surprisingly resonant to Genesis, but dating far earlier. The most famous of these is the Babylonian creation story *Enuma Elish*, dating from the early second millennium B.C.E. It opens with a primeval watery chaos in which three watery gods intermingle, including Tiamat, who gives birth to other gods. War breaks out among the gods, and the god Marduk kills Tiamat, separating her body into waters above and waters beneath, which he imprisons with iron bars. Light from the gods pierces darkness, dry land is separated from water, and Marduk establishes sun and moon to mark day and night. Humans are fashioned to be servants so that the gods can rest. The story is told on six tablets; on the seventh tablet, Marduk is crowned king of the gods and builds a palace, and the gods have a banquet.

  The language and images of this myth are detectable in Genesis 1:1–2:3: there are seven stages culminating in rest; creation proceeds by dividing waters and bringing order out of chaos; the sun and moon mark days and seasons. More important, however, are the differences, which reveal the point of the story in Genesis. There is only one God: the waters and heavenly bodies are not gods but mere creatures. There is no battle: creation is not a result of conflict and struggle. And humans are not slaves, but created for relationship with God.

Some other passages in the Bible, however, reflect the ancient creation myths more explicitly by alluding to God battling with a chaotic sea and with sea monsters. We can see similarities especially with the Canaanite version of the cosmic battle myth—discovered at Ugarit in Syria and dating from the middle of the second millennium B.C.E. Baal, the biblical "god of the Canaanites," was the storm god and Rider of the Clouds. He is challenged by the water god called Prince *Yamm* (Sea) and Judge *Nahar* (River)—lord of the primal chaotic subterranean waters (*Tehom*, the Deep). Baal defeats *Yamm* and becomes king of the gods. He builds a palace on the sacred mountain Zaphon. In another version, Baal also defeats a seven-headed sea monster named Leviathan/*Tannin*. We will see below the reverberations of this myth elsewhere in the Bible, but in Genesis 1, we need to recall that before creation there is the "Deep" (*Tehom*, Gen. 1:2), and among God's creations are the sea monsters (*Tannin*, Gen. 1:21).

Similarly, one can also detect the influence of ancient Near Eastern myths on the second creation story in Genesis. In particular, Genesis 2–3 and 6–8 reflects the broad outlines of the Mesopotamian myth of *Atrahasis* (eighteenth century B.C.E.): irrigation allows agriculture; gods originally work the soil; humans are molded from clay to work the land; marriage is instituted; humans anger the gods; humans are punished; a god causes a flood to destroy humans; a god instructs the human to build an ark; and after the flood the human offers sacrifice, reconciling gods to humans.

So far, then, we need to understand that the story of creation in Genesis uses the language of myth that was the common cultural currency (Enns 2012, 35–60). The most important difference has to do with questions of meaning—not the "how" but the "what for?" of creation.

Genesis 1–2: Biblical context

We have seen that Genesis begins with two different, but complementary stories of creation. These stories really serve as part of the prologue to the book, which extends until chapter 11. Genesis 1 presents an ideal of universal harmony among humans, the natural world, and God. There is no killing even for food

(Gen. 1:29–30). But human actions jeopardize all of this, and the result is alienation, antagonism, and violence. In the stories from Genesis 3 to 11, the world that God ordered devolves to chaos and disorder. God despairs the creation of humans and allows the primal waters of chaos to be unleashed, undoing creation; this is the flood of Genesis 6–9. The ideal harmony among humans, the natural world, and God is ruined.

The main story of Genesis starts in chapter 12 with Abraham, who is promised a land, many descendants, and blessing that will extend to all the families of the earth. That is, Abraham is somehow the answer to the problem of alienation that infects humanity. But Abraham's wife Sarah is barren, so this is really the story of a *creation of a people*. The focus of Genesis is telling the story of the creation of *this particular people*.

How do things look if we open the field of vision to the entire Hebrew Bible/Old Testament? What does the Bible as a whole teach about creation of the world and the origin of life? The short answer is…surprisingly little. Outside Genesis 1–2, there is almost no teaching in the Bible *about* creation of the world. Rather, creation is mostly assumed as a supporting theme.

After Genesis 1–2, the main treatment of creation is in Isaiah 40–55. These chapters were written in the sixth century B.C.E. during the exile to Babylon of the leaders of Judah, the remaining kingdom of the former nation of Israel. The prophet encourages the exiles that God will fulfill the promise to Abraham and restore the nation to its land. Israel's God, who saved Israel throughout history, is the God of creation (e.g., Isa. 42:5–6). The story of Moses leading the people out of Egypt to the Promised Land is presented as a *creation story*, the creation of Israel (Anderson 1984, 3–7): "[H]e who created you, O Jacob, he who formed you, O Israel: Do not fear, for I have redeemed you …" (Isa. 43:1, NRSV). This God can and will save Israel now, bringing Israel out of Babylon in a new creation (Isa. 43:14–16). That is, creation for this prophet is not about how God made the world in the distant past, but about how God acts in the present to save Israel, and what God will do in the future. Moreover, to describe God's saving actions in history he uses the language of the ancient creation myths where gods battle a cosmic dragon and bring the primeval sea of chaos under control. For example, in Isaiah 51, he presents the exodus story as a battle in which God slayed a dragon and dried up the sea (Isa. 51:9–10).

The prophet calls on God to do so again to return the exiles from Babylon. A similar use of this language of ancient creation myths is also found in several Psalms (e.g., Ps. 74 and 89); once again, the point is to describe God's saving actions in history, especially deliverance from Egypt and Babylon.

Psalm 104 and Job 38–41 offer two great meditations on creation. Both reflect the cosmology common in the ancient world with the sky as a roof to hold back the waters (Ps. 104:2–3 and Job 38:8–9) and the world as a disk built on pillars (Ps. 104:5–9) with gates and bars to hold back the chaotic primal sea (Job 38:8–11, 16–17). Both also allude to elements of the old myths: God battles the sea (Ps. 104:7 and Job 38:8) and the sea monster Leviathan (Ps. 104:26 and Job 41). The psalmist describes Yahweh like the storm god Baal who rides on the clouds (Ps. 104:3). Neither of these psalms shows any concern to teach about the origins of life or the "how" of creation. Rather, these meditations focus on the dependence of all life on God in the present (Anderson 1984, 11–14).

The New Testament contains even less *about* creation and reflects similar usage as the Old Testament. Creation reveals dependence on God (Rom. 1:19–20). The God who is worshiped is the creator (Rev. 10:6). The motif of creation of a people becomes the creation of a *new* people, Jew and Gentile (Eph. 2:10–15). The cosmic battle myth returns in Revelation: God creates a new heaven and earth where there is no more sea—that chaotic, threatening force (Rev. 21:1). The focus is not on how life came to be, but on the restoration of a good creation gone bad (Rom. 8:19–25). What about Adam, though? It is true that Adam appears in the genealogy of Israel in the Old Testament (1 Chron. 1:1) and of Jesus in the New Testament (Luke 3:38). Here Adam is treated as a historical figure in a lineage that includes at least some unmistakeably historical figures. However, the word *adam* simply means humankind. Genesis 1 tells of the creation of the human race ("God created humankind (*adam*) in his image ... male and female he created *them*," Gen. 1:27; cf. Gen. 5:1–2). To start a genealogy with "humanity" is a mythic way to tell a family story. Moreover, it is very common in the ancient world to ground the genealogy of a people in mythic ancestors. The concern of these genealogies is the creation of Israel, not the origin of all things.

Some argue that Adam must be a historical person because Paul compares Jesus to Adam (1 Cor. 15:22, 45–49; see also Rom. 5:12–14). Alluding to the creation of Adam from dust (Gen. 2:7; cf. 1 Cor. 15:45, 47), Paul treats Adam as a single ancestor of all humans, and Jesus as a new Adam who gives all humanity a second chance. This theological point, however, does not require a historical Adam. Paul also says that Jesus was the rock in the wilderness that supplied water for the Israelites in the time of Moses (1 Cor. 10:4; cf. Num. 20:7–12). In both places, his point is that Jesus is the source of spiritual life. (If we took Paul's identification of Jesus with the rock in the wilderness literally, we would have the humorous image that God gets angry with Moses for whacking Jesus with a stick; cf. Num. 20:11–12). In the end, Paul's comparison of Jesus to Adam is not to teach about the origin of life, but the creation of a new people in Christ: "Just as we have borne the image of the man of dust, we will also bear the image of the man of heaven" (1 Cor. 15:49).

In short, the Bible shows little interest in the mechanics of creation. When it does give an account of creation—Genesis 1:1–2:4—it borrows the language and imagery of myths, albeit drained of their lifeblood. Genesis is primarily interested in "Where did *we* come from? Who are *we* as people of God?" rather than "Where did humans come from? How did the world get here?" The same could be said for the Bible as a whole. The New Testament expands the scope of this people, but the usage and concerns are similar.

Reflections

The Bible as sacred scripture functions as an authoritative guide to faith for Christians. As a Christian with a long and broad immersion in the life and faith of multiple churches—both evangelical and mainline Protestant—I understand the power of these stories to challenge my own narrative. To mine the Bible for scientific data, however, or to treat it as a science or history book, is a false errand. Many religious leaders and denominations acknowledge that there is no conflict between religious faith and accepting evolution as a scientific explanation of the natural world—in various more and less helpful ways (National Council of Churches 2006; Pew 2009; 2013).

As a biblical scholar, I acknowledge that the Bible is an ancient collection of texts, rooted in specific cultures and reflecting worldviews far removed from our own. From studying how Jews and Christians have interpreted the Bible throughout history, I recognize that interpretation too is always rooted in specific cultures and worldviews. The Bible does interact with real historical events and persons, and with the real world of nature, but its understanding of these is commensurate with knowledge of the time. On these matters, the biblical writers show no greater accuracy than other ancient writers. More to the point, the Bible often blends myth with history and observation of the world precisely because its main message is not about the observable facts of the world, but what one *cannot* observe, with questions of meaning and how to live.

Evolution and other scientific theories are based on evidence and rigorous testing of hypotheses—an enterprise entirely different from the reflections of faith. I believe that the scientific investigation of evolution and its conclusions should be taught in schools, unfettered by constraints of how it challenges ancient or current worldviews. The Bible contributes nothing to this enterprise, neither data nor method. It does, however, teach us to value all life and the world in which we live.

Works Cited

Anderson, Bernard. "Introduction: Mythopoeic and Theological Dimensions of Biblical Creation Faith." In *Creation in the Old Testament*, edited by Bernhard W. Anderson, pp. 1–24. Issues in Religion and Theology 6. Philadelphia: Fortress, 1984.

Berkman, Michael and Plutzer, Eric. *Evolution, Creationism, and the Battle to Control America's Classrooms*. New York: Cambridge University Press, 2010.

Berkman, Michael and Plutzer, Eric. "Enablers of Doubt: How Future Teachers Learn to Negotiate the Evolution Wars in Their Classrooms," *The Annals of the American Academy of Political and Social Science* 658 (2015): 253–270.

Boyle, Tara, Farden, Vicki and Godoy, Maria. "Teaching Evolution: A State-by-State Debate." *National Public Radio*. December 20, 2005. http://www.npr.org/templates/story/story.php?storyId=4630737 (accessed March 12, 2016).

Enns, Peter. *The Evolution of Adam: What the Bible Does and Doesn't Say about Human Origins*. Grand Rapids, MI: Brazos, 2012.

Henderson, Ben. "Belief in Evolution Up since 2004." YouGov.com. July 22, 2013. https://today.yougov.com/news/2013/07/22/belief-in -evolution-up-since–2004/ (accessed March 11, 2016).

Lebo, Lauri. "The Scopes Strategy: Creationists Try New Tactics to Promote Anti-Evolutionary Teaching in Public Schools." *Scientific American*. February 28, 2011. http://www.scientificamerican.com/ article/scopes-creationism-education/ (accessed March 11, 2016).

Masci, David. "The Social and Legal Dimensions of the Evolution Debate in the U.S." Pew Research Center, Washington, D.C. February 4, 2009, updated February 3, 2014. http://www.pewforum.org/2009/02/04/ the-social-and-legal-dimensions-of-the-evolution-debate-in-the-us/ (accessed March 10, 2016).

National Council of Churches. "Science, Religion, and the Teaching of Evolution in Public School Science Classes." The National Council of Churches Committee on Public Education and Literacy, 2006. http:// www.ucc.org/justice/public-education/pdfs/evolutionbrochurefinal.pdf (accessed March 10, 2016).

Newport, Frank. "In US, 46% Hold Creationist View of Human Origins." Gallup Poll. June 1, 2012. http://www.gallup.com/poll/155003/Hold -Creationist-View-Human-Origins.aspx (accessed March 11, 2016).

Pearce, Matt. "U.S. Rep. Paul Broun: Evolution a Lie 'From the Pit of Hell.'" *Los Angeles Times*. October 7, 2012. http://articles.latimes .com/2012/oct/07/nation/la-na-nn-paul-broun-evolution- hell-20121007 (accessed March 12, 2016).

Pew. "Religious Groups' Views on Evolution." Pew Research Center, Washington, D.C. February 4, 2009; updated February 3, 2014. http:// www.pewforum.org/2009/02/04/religious-groups-views-on-evolution/ (accessed March 10, 2016).

Pew. "Public's Views on Human Evolution." Pew Research Center, Washington, D.C. December 30, 2013. http://www.pewforum .org/2013/12/30/publics-views-on-human-evolution/ (accessed March 10, 2016).

Sarna, Nahum M. *Genesis*. Jewish Publication Society Torah Commentary Series. Ann Arbor, MI: JPS, 2001.

Scott, Eugenie C. *Evolution vs. Creationism: An Introduction*, 2nd edn. Westport, CO: Greenwood Press, 2009.

"Third G.O.P. Debate." *The New York Times*. June 5, 2007. http://nyti .ms/1UlOafZ (accessed March 10, 2016).

PART TWO

The Bible in Historical Political Debate

9

Tracing the Use of the Bible in Colonial Land Claims in North America

Judith H. Newman

Eureka! In 1830, gold was discovered in the United States—not in California, but in northwest Georgia, in part of the 5.2 million acres that were then Cherokee land. The state legislature promptly passed a law claiming all the gold mines to be the property of the state. Within a month, Georgia had authorized the seizure of all Cherokee land turning it over to be distributed to white settlers.

In order to prevent any countermeasures, the state also prohibited the Cherokees from assembling on their lands and from passing their own laws. The results of these state actions would spark a national debate, not only about states' rights versus federal laws, but also about the fate of Indian nations in the expanding United States (Banner 2005). Within the span of eight years, the Cherokees, along with other tribes of the deep south, the Choctaw, Chickasaw, Muskogee, and Seminole, would be removed, trudging along a Trail of Tears to newly designated Indian territories west of the Mississippi. Of the 16,000 Cherokees alone who made the 1,200 mile trip, the death toll is estimated at 4,000.

The events of the 1830s were in no sense isolated in American history, but were rooted in a long-standing tradition of European claims on territories in the New World. Imagery from the Bible propped up some of these European claims to the land, already settled by indigenous peoples. Christian settlers often understood themselves as a new Israel confronting the native Canaanites. Native American lives and cultures were at risk if they did not accept the new religion (Warrior 1995). The land was at once the untamed Wilderness and a prospective Eden, if it was cultivated and settled in the proper Anglo-American way. Such biblical interpretation was intertwined with the cultural self-understanding of the European settlers as a superior race. Their Christian religion could serve the purpose of "civilizing" people they often described as "savages," considered less than human because of their nomadic way of life and religious beliefs.

Thus, the first "immigrant problem" in North America was the uninvited arrival of European explorers and settlers, at least from the perspective of the continent's native inhabitants. The indigenous peoples on the new continents did not have the power to control the influx of new people entering their lands. The European newcomers would bring "guns, germs, and steel," eventually resulting in a decimation of the native populations because of disease and death during warfare from more powerful kinds of weapons (Diamond 2005). They would also bring with them cultural attitudes shaped by their Christian beliefs and practices.

Beginning with a trickle after the exploratory ventures of Christopher Columbus to the New World and leading into large resettlements in the time of the colonial era, the newcomers were motivated by a mission to convert the natives to Christianity, conquest of peoples, and acquisition of lands in equal measure. The story of how the Bible and Christianity were involved in legitimating the dispossession of indigenous peoples in the Americas is a complicated one and cannot be told fully here. We can just tease out a few strands in that intricate web of history.

The Bible in the age of empires

To discuss the use of the Bible in dispossessing indigenous peoples in the Americas requires backing up to a time well before the United States and Canada became independent nations in 1776 and 1867. These were the days of the growing European empires, beginning when Christopher Columbus launched his first voyage under the sponsorship of the monarchs of the Spanish Empire in the fateful year 1492. Columbus himself was motivated by a devout Christian faith and he was greatly shaped by scripture. Toward the end of his life, Columbus wrote a book that chronicled his life, *Libro de las Profecias* (*Book of Prophecies*). His book makes clear the extent to which Columbus saw his voyage as fulfilling biblical prophecy. He read the Bible and Christian commentators to create a depiction of how the world would end and understood his own role in exploring new lands in that light. In the words of one historian of Christianity: "Millennial [apocalyptic] readings of American history did not begin with Jonathan Edwards in the 1740s or Dwight L. Moody in the 1870s; they inspired the voyages of 1492. How to apply prophecy to current events remains an issue to ponder" (Marty 1992).

Columbus would complete his last mission when King Ferdinand and Queen Isabella refused to fund his fourth expedition, but he would be succeeded by many Spanish conquistadors in the sixteenth century. They were intent on expanding their dominion over foreign lands, acquiring new territories to gain wealth, and requiring tributes from the conquered natives. The first European explorers and settlers brought a potent weapon with them in addition to muskets and rifles: the Bible as they interpreted it through their own European lenses and religious cultures. In speeches and sermons, in laws and lore, the Bible was invoked in many ways during precolonial and colonial days.

The doctrine of discovery

The reign of Isabella and Ferdinand was marked by a period of religious prejudice as Jews and Muslims, tolerated for centuries on the Iberian Peninsula, were persecuted. Jews were forced to convert to Catholic Christianity or be expelled in 1492. In the decades that followed, the Muslims were also cast out. This religious fervor extended to the new territories across the seas. In 1493, Pope Alexander VI published the bull *Inter Caetera*. The Pope "by the authority of Almighty God conferred upon us in blessed Peter and of the vicarship of Jesus Christ" would grant monarchs the ability to claim foreign lands under the condition that the inhabitants be converted. Implicit in this invocation of pope, in unbroken succession from the disciple Peter, stands the well-known words of Jesus to his favorite disciple in Matthew 16:18: "And I tell you, you are Peter, and on this rock I will build my church." In addition to establishing the ultimate divine authority of royal claims to the land, the papal proclamation made provision that any lands discovered in the western hemisphere that were "not previously possessed by any Christian king or prince" would henceforth be divided between Portugal and Spain.

Papal claims to indigenous lands did not go unchallenged. Priest and professor Franciscus de Victoria, chief advisor to the king, argued strongly against them on the basis of natural law. In his influential lectures at the University of Salamanca "On the Indians Lately Discovered," he asserted that native people had natural rights to the land. In the following centuries, disputes would occur over distinctions between rightful occupation, possession, and ownership of the land, but Victoria's argument loosened papal claims. It allowed other European Christian nations to make their own land claims in newly discovered regions (MacMillan 2006). This Doctrine of Discovery, the principle that became the first kind of international law, undergirds both American and Canadian policy toward native populations to this day.

The Spanish requirement to convert or be subject to violence

As a result of the papal proclamation, the Spanish monarchs formulated a long text used in the conquering of the new lands, called the *Requirimiento* or Requirement, which led to a necessary ritual before taking possession of the land. When explorers conquered new territories, the first obligation was the reading of the Requirement to natives before hostilities or "just war" could legally begin. The text was read in Spanish to people who did not speak the language. It might be read at night at the edge of a sleeping native settlement. Captains might read it while on a ship before disembarking, only to send out a mission to enslave natives with its leaders shouting the war cry "Santiago" before attacking. If the natives did not accept the authority of the Catholic Church and the Spanish monarchs, then Spain understood itself to be legitimately waging war on them (Miller 2006).

But where did the tradition of conversion or subjugation found in the Catholic Requirement come from? At its heart, the Requirement ultimately stems from an Islamic-inspired order that required non-Muslims to submit to Islam or endure attack (Seed 1995). When Muslims debated Jews and Christians in medieval Spain, they frequently tried to demonstrate how their religion lay in continuity with Judaism and Christianity. To legitimate their practice of *jihad*, or warfare, they often quoted a text from Deuteronomy that describes Israelite conduct in the event of wars (Fritsch 1930):

> When you draw near to a town to fight against it, offer it terms of peace. If it accepts your terms of peace and surrenders to you, then all the people in it shall serve you at forced labor. If it makes war against you, then you shall besiege it; and when the Lord your God gives it into your hand, you shall put all its males to the sword. You may, however, take as your booty, the women, the children, livestock, and everything else in the town, all its spoil. You may enjoy the spoil of your enemies, which the Lord your God has given you. Thus you shall treat all the towns that are very far from you, which are not towns of the nations here. But as for the towns of these peoples that the Lord your God is giving you as an inheritance, you must not let anything that breathes remain alive. (Deut. 20:10–16)

The passage from Deuteronomy presents itself as part of the laws that Moses presents to the Israelites as they entered the Promised Land to conquer its indigenous inhabitants. Most biblical scholars believe it actually stems from a later time and place, presenting an idealized account of a war that may have never occurred in that manner.

It is this idealized version of war that inspired the Spanish conquistadors. As Christians, they thought of themselves as the new Israel, having displaced the Jews as the "true Israel." Now they would conquer the inhabitants of the New World, the "towns that are very far from you," that they believed God had given to them. Forced labor, slaughter of the males, and capture of the females, children, and booty were all allowed, according to Deuteronomy. This Spanish interpretation assumes that the law no longer relates just to the history of the ancient land of Israel during the time of Moses. The war practice is seen as valid in the present in lands far away from the Holy Land. Such were the contortions sometimes required in adapting biblical texts to new contexts.

The Spanish and Portuguese vision of colonization was one in which dominating and subjugating people even while they remained on the land was central. The Spaniard Bartolomé de las Casas would become the most prominent religious voice arguing against his country's treatment of native peoples. An early colonial settler of the West Indies, he initially accepted the colonial perspective that allowed for slavery. Over time, he became increasingly disenchanted with the abuses. De las Casas joined the Dominican order and a turning point came in 1514, when las Casas was studying a passage from his Roman Catholic Bible in preparation for a Pentecost sermon. Through his reading of Ecclesiasticus 34:18–22, de las Casas became convinced that the Spanish treatment of natives in the New World was not only wrong, but illegal (Brading 1997). He would go on to write *A Short Account of the Destruction of the Indies* that catalogued the sins of the Spanish colonialists. Because of his ideas about equality of persons, he is considered the originator of the modern concept of universal human rights.

Like the Spanish and Portuguese monarchs, the French, English, and Dutch were also intent on exploring and exploiting the new lands based on the Doctrine of Discovery. They would establish a new precedent that was tacitly agreed to by the great empires. Religious claims for the new lands rooted in the Bible cannot be disentangled from ethnocentric theories of race and empire. The idea of the superiority of Christian European cultures and the "white race" went hand in hand with their understanding of "civilization." This was true even as Protestant groups, protesting the political and religious persecution they found in Europe, began to seek foreign shores of the New World in order to find free expression for their religious beliefs and practices. Yet the various nations had distinct cultures. Early English settlers, the Puritans in New England, and the Anglicans further down the coast in Virginia were intent not so much on conquering and subduing the *people* they encountered, as in claiming their *lands* through cultivation, possession, and settlement.

The Puritans in the New Israel

Eager to escape the restrictions placed upon him by Anglicans and Roman Catholics in England because of his Puritan faith, John Winthrop penned an idealistic sermon aboard the ship *Arbella* on his way to the Massachusetts Bay Colony. In "A Model of

Christian Charity," Winthrop drew on more than Matthew's gospel in crafting his vision for his new covenant community in the new world. He would also affirm that "the God of Israel is among us." He closed his sermon with the exhortation from Moses to the people of Israel in Deuteronomy 30 to obey God's commandments and laws, so that by obedience they might form a new covenant. Like the Spanish Requirement of a century prior, Winthrop would understand himself as part of a new Israel. Now this new Moses was headed toward the Promised Land of New England, with a destiny to pursue there in planting a new settlement. Like the ancient Israelites, some colonists would choose the wrong way and stray from the path of life.

The first people to be enslaved in New England were not Africans, but Native Americans captured during wars with the first settlers during the colonial period. The most infamous and decisive war in the history of the Puritan settlement was the Pequot war of 1637–1638. This war pitted the powerful Pequot tribe against the Puritan settlers and their native allies and Pequot rivals, the Narragansetts and the Mohegans. Tensions between the Pequots and the Puritans had been building for years, but culminated over the Pequot killing of a trader. Colonial demands for avenging his death resulted in war. A series of near massacres by the Puritans and their Indian allies in Pequot villages near what are now the towns of Mystic, Stonington, and Fairfield, Connecticut, left the Pequots decimated. Surviving Pequots were sold into slavery, though some escaped to nearby tribes. The brutal destruction of the Pequots made a deep impression on other tribes and cleared the way for further Puritan expansion and settlement.

Soldiers who had participated in the war wrote to Governor Winthrop to ask for their share of the human booty: "There is a little Squa that Steward Calacot desireth," wrote one. And another: "Lieutenant Damport also desireth one, to witt, a tall one with three strokes upon her stomach...." (C.S. Manegold 2010a). Some of these enslaved natives were shipped to the West Indies and traded for "cotton, and tobacco and Negroes," according to Winthrop's journal. By the next year, the Massachusetts Court of Assistants ruled "the Governor had leave to keep a Narragansett Indian and his wife" (C.S. Manegold 2010a). Indeed, there would be slaves on Winthrop's homestead, the 600 hundred acre farm

Ten Hills, not only during his day, but for the next 150 years under subsequent owners.

The Puritans did not escape the strident criticism of other Christians in the New World. Most famous is the disapproval of the English colonist Thomas Morton, who brought a lawsuit against the Massachusetts Bay Colony. He derided the strict authoritarian rule of the Puritan government in the colonies as well as their near genocide of the natives. His leadership in founding the settlement Merry Mount, well to the south of the Puritans, was based on amicable relations with the Algonquins. In 1637, Morton would become well known after publishing his three-volume work *New English Canaan*. Although remaining colonial in spirit and using the same "new Israel" typology that his fellow colonists the Puritans embraced, he envisioned a New Canaan in which natives might live and flourish together.

Cultivating the wilderness in the New England

Understanding America as the New Israel was a central theme in the English self-understanding in the New World, but other biblical passages reinforced colonial land claims. The most frequent verse of scripture used to legitimize possession in the new colonies was Genesis 1:28: "God blessed them, and God said to them, 'Be fruitful and multiply, and fill the earth and subdue it; and have dominion over the fish of the sea and over the birds of the air and over every living thing that moves upon the earth.'" Most readers of this verse through the ages have understood the injunction to "be fruitful and multiply" as a mandate for the first two humans to reproduce (Cohen 1989). The English were unique in their way of connecting Genesis 1:28 to agriculture.

The association was rooted in a medieval Anglo-Saxon folk ritual that was a cure for infertile soil. The sod would be lifted up and water sprinkled over four parts of the soil. "Be fruitful," "and multiply, "and fill" "the earth" was recited, while holy water was sprinkled over it. The Lord's Prayer was also recited (Seed 1995). The association with fertility of the soil and agriculture became part of England's distinctive *cultural* understanding of the verse.

This interpretation would be extended more generally to how land should be used and possessed from the perspective of the early English settlers and colonial advocates. The emphasis on agrarian use and cultivation was central to establishing English rights and limiting native property rights to areas that the English wanted to settle (Seed 2001).

Writing from England in hopes of encouraging more colonies to be planted abroad, clergyman Richard Eburne wrote: "It was God's express commandment to Adam that he should fill the earth and subdue it. By virtue of which charter he and his have ever since had the privilege to spread themselves from place to place and to have, hold, occupy, and enjoy any region or country whatsoever which they should find either not preoccupied" (Eburne 1962 [1624, 31]). For Eburne as with his fellow colonialists, the discovered land on which natives might hunt and gather was not considered fully occupied. Building houses and participating in agriculture established ownership (cf. Banner 2005).

The language could be found in new colonial laws, which routinely cited scripture. When a Massachusetts court was deciding which lands the natives might possess, the determination was made on the basis of the primeval natural law to be found in Genesis: "what lands any of the Indians, within this jurisdiction, have by possession or improvement, by subduing of the same, they have just right thereto, according to that Genesis 1:28, 9:1; Psalms 115, 116" (Cronon 2003, 63). Native inhabitants might thus also lay claim to possessing the land, but only if they improved it according to English standards. In English villages, improving occurred through enclosure with fences, permanent domestic buildings, and agrarian cultivation through fertilizing and planting crops. Nonetheless, according to the Doctrine of Discovery, the original European nation that had "found" the land held ultimate dominion and sovereignty.

For the native inhabitants of the Americas, the land was not created for humanity, humanity was created to honor the land. As Chief Seattle would affirm in his famous oration: "Every part of this soil is sacred in the estimation of my people." The Creator had made it to be shared (Cherry 1998, 136). By contrast, the practice of treating land as property to be bought and sold was a distinctively European import. The philosopher and government official John Locke was instrumental in formalizing the English understanding of the possession of land in civil terms. In his influential work *Two Treatises of Government*, written at the end of the seventeenth century, he would establish the definition of land as property: "As much Land as a Man Tills, Plants, Improves, Cultivates, and can use the Product of, so much is his Property." According to Locke, the natives did not possess property rights "for want of improving it by Labour" (Banner 2005, 46).

The emphasis on agrarian use and cultivation was central to establishing English rights and limiting native property rights to areas that the English wanted to settle (Seed 2001). While there were multiple conflicting perspectives on law during the early colonial period (Benton 2002), toward the end in 1763, King George III issued a Royal Proclamation, which made a clear ruling about land. The Crown asserted the claim to dominions and territories to the east of the Mississippi through the Doctrine of Discovery principle. As the European Christian power that had "discovered" the region, the king alone had the power to grant land titles; it was not possible for private individuals to purchase aboriginal land without royal permission. This would set a precedent for sovereign claims to dominion over native lands that the young United States and the Confederation of Canada would also follow.

Andrew Jackson and Manifest Destiny

The spirit of Manifest Destiny permeated the new republic in the nineteenth century. With roots in Winthrop's Puritan vision of a New Israel with a divinely ordained providential destiny in the new land, America's sense of purpose was galvanized. This destiny was now expressed through "geographical predestination" as the new country set its sights on expanding ever-westward (Cherry 1998).

The most significant public policy decision of the century relied not on biblical texts as had colonial laws, but affirmed the long-standing Doctrine of Discovery. In the 1823 Supreme Court decision *Johnson v. M'Intosh*, Chief Justice John Marshall ruled that the discovering nation had "ultimate dominion of the land, the power to grant the soil, while yet in possession of the natives" (Banner 2005, 182). Natives might retain possession and occupancy, but they were not the land's owners. The results meant that the federal government or its member states could give land grants on native lands to white settlers who then might become owners.

The nineteenth century would thus prove decisive and devastating for Native American claims to their original territories. The story of the Georgia "gold rush" with which we began was just one episode in the sequence of events that spelled a new era. Native peoples experienced the signing of treaties by tribal leaders, often in the face of disagreement among tribal members; their removal from their ancestral lands; the institution of the reservation system; and allotment. Treaties were often signed after warfare and a first nations' loss, when the terms of the treaty could be dictated to tribal chiefs to the advantage of the United States.

The government was intent on assimilating natives to a Euro-American way of life, with settlement and farming as the goal. President Andrew Jackson was forceful and blunt in articulating this aim. Speaking to the Congress after the passage of the Indian Removal Act of 1830, President Andrew Jackson hoped that among the benefits to the natives, it might cause them "to cast off their savage habits and become an interesting, civilized, and Christian community…. And is it supposed that the wandering savage has a stronger attachment to his home than the settled, civilized Christian?" (Jackson 1830). Not only were the Christian religion and the white race superior to the religions and cultures of the natives, but to Jackson's understanding, settlement was infinitely more "civilized" than the nomadic, hunter–gatherer way of life of aboriginals.

The younger nation to the north would share a similar pattern of land expropriation, though both English and French colonial powers had shaped the north. Canada, after its Confederation in 1867, sought lessons from the United States. John A. MacDonald, the first Prime Minister of Canada, commissioned Nicholas Flood Davin, a reporter and politician, to investigate the industrial boarding schools for natives operating then in the United States. In his report, Davin would observe that "the race is in its childhood" and recommend that Canada institute a similar schooling system to teach agriculture and animal husbandry alongside Christianity.

From the 1880s on, Canada began to establish residential schools in part to fulfill their commitment to provide education for aboriginal children. The schools were run by Roman Catholic, Anglican, Presbyterian, Methodist, and United Church of Canada organizations. Religious instruction was emphasized, though the role played by the Bible depended on the church body in charge. The Alberni Indian Residential School on Victoria Island, British Columbia, was run by the Presbyterians and stressed memorization. Principal James Motion reported in 1904, "Three children under ten have memorized one hundred verses of Scripture and received certificates; five have memorized the Shorter Catechism, eight others have memorized two hundred verses of Scripture" (Motion 1904).

With the passage of the Indian Act in 1920, the government could compel children to attend residential school. Native children were taken from their families, some even as young as four, and required to attend these residential schools, with or without parental consent. Many students were forbidden to speak their native languages or practice their culture. Others were subject to physical, sexual, and emotional abuse. Enrollment peaked in the mid-1950s and the last residential school did not close until 1995. A growing recognition of the harm done by these schools led Prime Minister Stephen Harper in 2008 to issue a formal apology from the government of Canada for the damage done through this attempt to "kill the Indian in the child." While Christian missionary activity may have been well intentioned, and many natives accepted Christianity, the result was a decidedly mixed legacy in missionary scorn for native ways and peoples.

Up to this point, the chapter has placed in the foreground the perspective of European settlers of North America. It seems only right to shift viewpoints and close with the words of Sa-go-ye-wat-ha, or Red Jacket, a Seneca chief and great orator of the Six Nations. The response he gave at a council in 1805 in Buffalo to a young missionary serves to illuminate the larger issues not only of this chapter but of those in this entire volume:

> Brother, … we understand that your religion is written in a book. If it was intended for us as well as you, why has not the Great Spirit given to us—and not only to us, but to our forefathers—the knowledge of that book, with the means of understanding it rightly? We only know what you tell us about it. How shall we know when to believe, being so often deceived by the white people? Brother, you say there is but one way to worship and serve the Great Spirit. If there is but one religion, why do you white people differ so much about it? Why not all agree, as you can all read the book? (McLuhan 1971, 61)

Works Cited

Banner, Stuart. *How the Indians Lost Their Land: Law and Power on the Frontier*. Cambridge, MA: Harvard University Press, 2005.

Benton, Lauren. *Law and Colonial Cultures: Legal Regimes in World History, 1400–1900*. New York: Cambridge University Press, 2002.

Brading, David A. "Prophet and Apostle: Bartolomé de las Casas and the Spiritual Conquest of America." In *Christianity and Missions, 1450–1800. An Expanding World: The European Impact on World History, 1450–1800*, edited by J.S. Cummins. Vol. 28, 117–138. Aldershot: Ashgate Publishing, 1997.

Bremer, Francis J. *John Winthrop: America's Forgotten Founding Father*. New York: Oxford University Press, 2005.

Cherry, Conrad (ed.). *God's New Israel: Religious Interpretations of American Destiny*. Revised and updated edition. Chapel Hill: University of North Carolina Press, 1998.

Cohen, Jeremy. *"Be Fertile and Increase, Fill the Earth and Master It": The Ancient and Medieval Career of a Biblical Text*. Ithaca, NY: Cornell University Press, 1989.

Cronon, William. *Changes in the Land: Indians, Colonists, and the Ecology of New England*. Revised edition. New York: Hill and Wang, 2003.

Cushman, Robert. "Reasons and Considerations Touching the Lawfulness of Removing out of England into the Parts of America (1622)." In *The Puritans in America: A Narrative Anthology*, edited by Andrew Delbanco and Alan Heimert. Cambridge, MA: Harvard University Press, 1985.

Diamond, Jared. *Guns, Germs, and Steel: The Fates of Human Societies*. New York: W.W. Norton, 2005.

Eburne, Richard. *A Plaine Pathway to Plantations*, edited by Louis B. Wright. Ithaca, NY: Cornell University Press, 1962 [1624].

Fritsch, Erdmann. *Islam und Christentum im mittelalter: Beiträge zur geschichte der muslimischen polemic gegen das Christentum in arabischer sprache*. Breslau: Müller, 1930.

Jackson, Andrew. Transcript of President Andrew Jackson's Message to Congress "On Indian Removal," 1830. http://www.ourdocuments .gov/doc.php?flash=true&doc=25&page=transcript (accessed February 29, 2016).

MacMillan, Ken. *Sovereignty and Possession in the English New World: The Legal Foundations of Empire, 1576–1640*. Cambridge: Cambridge University Press, 2006.

Manegold, C.S. "New England's Scarlet 'S' for Slavery." *The Boston Globe*. January 18, 2010a.

Manegold, C.S. *Ten Hills Farm: The Forgotten Story of Slavery in the North*. Princeton, NJ: Princeton University Press, 2010b.

Marty, Martin E. "The Clamor over Columbus." *Christianity Today* 35
    (1992). http://www.christianitytoday.com/history/issues/issue-35/
    clamor-over-columbus.html (accessed February 29, 2016).
Miller, Robert J. *Native America, Discovered and Conquered: Thomas
    Jefferson, Lewis & Clark, and Manifest Destiny.* Westport, CT:
    Praeger, 2006.
Miller, Robert J., Ruru, Jacinta, Behrendt, Larissa and Lindberg, Tracey.
    *Discovering Indigenous Lands: The Doctrine of Discovery in the
    English Colonies.* New York: Oxford University Press, 2010.
Motion, James. "Motion to the Secretary General of Indian Affairs."
    July 28, 1904. http://thechildrenremembered.ca/school-locations/
    alberni/ (accessed February 29, 2016).
Reagan, Ronald. "Election Eve Address: 'A Vision for America.'"
    November 1980. http://www.presidency.ucsb.edu/ws/?pid=85199
Seed, Patricia. *American Pentimento: The Invention of Indians and
    the Pursuit of Riches.* Minneapolis, MN: University of Minnesota
    Press, 2001.
Seed, Patricia. *Ceremonies of Possession in Europe's Conquest of the New
    World 1492–1640.* New York: Cambridge University Press, 1995.
Seed, Patricia. "Taking Possession and Reading Texts: Establishing the
    Authority of Overseas Empires." *William and Mary Quarterly* 49
    (1992): 183–209.
Touch the Earth: A Self-Portrait of Indian Existence, edited by
    T.C. McLuhan. New York: Promontory Press, 1971.
Truth and Reconciliation Commission of Canada, Final Report. http://
    www.trc.ca/websites/trcinstitution/index.php?p=3
Warrior, Robert. "A Native American Perspective: Canaanites, Cowboys,
    and Indians." In *Voices from the Margin: Interpreting the Bible in the
    Third World,* edited by R.S. Sugirtharajah. New York and London:
    Orbis/SPCK, 1995.

10

The Bible, Slavery, and Political Debate

Emerson B. Powery

U.S. slavery, as a social institution, is no longer debated publicly in the political arena. Occasionally, it appears in the news as a point of interest related to some other contemporary phenomenon. In a recent exit poll survey, nearly 20 percent of Donald Trump supporters disapproved of President Lincoln's Emancipation Proclamation, which freed enslaved persons in southern states in rebellion against the federal government (Vavreck 2016). When this exit poll data is combined with a larger survey, it is difficult to discern whether one out of five people reacted negatively to the freeing of enslaved African-Americans or whether they thought the President's proclamation was an act of executive overreach (YouGov Poll 2016). If the latter was their primary concern, their dissatisfaction probably had more to do with the current President's own executive actions than with the sixteenth President's political maneuvering in the middle of the nineteenth century. However, even this position still betrays a certain lack of historical sensitivity to what is typically considered a moment that corrected one of the country's greatest injustices.

This story is the anomaly. Antebellum slavery usually appears in today's political headlines only as a major point of comparison, in which everyone would (presumably) acknowledge the gravity of our country's past mistake. It is assumed that people today—if they lived in the antebellum world—would have opposed human bondage. When running for the Republican Party's nomination, Ben Carson, for example, could compare slavery to abortion rights or the Affordable health-care reform, assuming that his audience would recognize the rightness of the abolitionist cause. On the former issue, Carson explained his analogy: "During slavery, a lot of slave-owners thought they had the right to do whatever they wanted to that slave, anything that they chose. And what if the abolitionists had said, 'I don't believe in slavery, but you guys do whatever you want'? Where would we be?" (Zurcher 2015).

Recalling the issue of slavery is not isolated to the discourse of one political party. Democratic Senator and 2016 presidential candidate Bernie Sanders was recently taken to task in *The Atlantic* (Coates 2016) for his refusal to consider reparations for the ancestors of the enslaved. Sanders called the proposal for financial restitution "very divisive" (Scott 2016).

The nineteenth-century context

Over 150 years ago, slavery was a (or, perhaps, *the*) major political issue that divided politicians, citizens, and ecclesial organizations. In March 1865, President Lincoln addressed the nation in his second inaugural address, a political speech that contained some of the most religious rhetoric in presidential history. In it, Lincoln claimed, "Both read the same Bible and pray to the same God" (Basler 1946). Despite Lincoln's words to reconcile disputing parties and warring factions nearing the end of the Civil War, his observation concedes the point that religion—and the Bible, in particular—had much to do with a person's view of the peculiar institution of slavery. But whose side was the Bible on?

The "Compromise of 1850" was a major turning point leading up to the Civil War. Organized by Henry Clay (a senator from Kentucky) and Daniel Webster (a senator from Massachusetts), Congress decided to pass this "compromise." It included the admission of California into the Union as a *free* state and the Fugitive Slave Act of 1850. The latter law required all citizens to assist in capturing so-called fugitives who had escaped into free territories. Abolitionists protested this concession. The government approved this effort as a political strategy to maintain the bonds of the Union in 1850.

This political negotiation received strong endorsement from some of the leading biblical scholars in the north. One example makes the point well. Moses Stuart, arguably the most prominent biblical scholar of his day, published a pamphlet called *Conscience and Constitution*. In this treatise, he argued in favor of a gradualist position for emancipation, in which southern slaveholders would voluntarily release their enslaved property. He was weary of the attack of "radical" abolitionists against his senator (Webster) and the Union as a whole. He also questioned the southern institution of human bondage because it failed to apply biblical principles in its practice. Although Stuart opposed maintaining the practice in perpetuity, he did not condemn slavery as sinful since the Bible neglected to denounce it outright.

Against those who would abolish slavery immediately, Stuart argued that the Bible supported a pro-slavery stance. From the patriarch Moses to Jesus, the Bible never prohibited holding humans in bondage. As a unionist, he claimed that "Universal and immediate emancipation would be little short of insanity" and that the anti-Bible position radical abolitionists took would initiate a war (Stuart 1850, 112). He was concerned as much with the authority of the Bible's position as he was the Union's stability.

Of particular interest—in light of the 1850 compromise—was Deuteronomy 23:15: "Thou shalt not deliver unto his master the servant which is escaped from his master unto thee" (KJV). The "fugitive" of Deuteronomy 23:15, according to Stuart, was a reference to the non-Israelite slave, who should receive a safe haven. All Hebrew slaves who escaped, on the other hand, should be returned to their fellow Hebrew masters (Stuart 1850). Centuries later, even Paul would send Onesimus back to Philemon, a fellow believer (Phlm. 1:12). In the same way, many would argue that black escapees should be returned to their "Christian" masters in the South, since "these States are not *heathen*" (Stuart 1850, 31–32; author's emphasis). Stuart's support of Webster's (and Clay's) compromise provisions influenced directly his interpretive conclusions. The literary and historical context of Deuteronomy is less clear on the ethnic background of the escapee. Most biblical scholars today agree that the "fugitive" in the context of Deuteronomy probably referred to an enslaved foreigner (Tigay 1996, 215).

However, *in favor of* the cause of emancipation, Stuart asserted that if, following the laws of Moses, slavery was still practiced, then citizens should also "insist on the liberty of polygamy and concubinage" (Stuart 1850, 36–37). Those positions were clearly enforced in ancient Israel. Most abolitionists, including Stuart, believed that the spirit of the Gospel was the new "supreme law" for Christian living. Along with others opposed to antebellum enslavement, gradual emancipationists found the practices of the peculiar institution in the South to be incompatible with a biblical approach to human bondage. To hinder access to education, marriage, and family life was an immoral way to treat one's "neighbor." Abolitionists of all stripes would often acknowledge the sexual abuse that enslaved, female bodies suffered (Stuart 1850). The words of Jesus—"do unto others as you would have them do unto you" (Matt. 7:12)—were often summoned to speak against such offenses. Yet, as a product of his time and culture, Stuart did not believe that this darker-skinned neighbor should actually become a fellow citizen in white communities. Rather he thought that blacks would need to be colonized in the same manner as Native Americans (Stuart 1850). Many northern whites opposed amalgamation, that is, the social intermingling of different racial groups. Even President Lincoln's original draft of the Emancipation Proclamation included a clause for the colonization of African-Americans. Whether and when Lincoln relinquished this idea is debated (Franklin 1994). For many gradual emancipationists, in defense of the Bible's authority, Christians could be slaveholders. Slavery was not a biblical sin! What no Christian slaveholder should do, however, was to keep the enslaved in a state of ignorance. Permanent slavery, therefore, was a "sin."

The Bible and slavery

Biblical support for human bondage was straightforward. Slavery was universally practiced in the ancient world, and evidence for its existence is present throughout the biblical story. The story of Genesis includes many references to slaves and masters (cf. Gen. 9:25–27; 12:16; 16:1; 17:12–13; 20:8; 30:43). The laws of ancient Israel assume the presence of enslaved bodies among the people of Israel (cf. Lev. 25:44–46). While Israel celebrated her very beginnings in terms of liberation from Egyptian oppression and enslavement, this memory of the Exodus event did *not* lead Israel's leaders to establish a land free of slaves. This memory exercised a more limited and occasional influence, such as stopping the sale of fellow Hebrew slaves to other groups (Lev. 25:39–43), advocating for "fair" payment when Hebrew slaves departed (Deut. 15:13–15), or, possibly, caring for "fugitive" slaves (Deut. 23:15–16). But in light of this collective memory, it is clear that Israel did not endorse abolition.

Ancient Israelite slavery continued into the Greco-Roman period. Early Christian house churches included "free" and "slave" within the developing Christian communities (e.g., Gal. 3:28; Col. 3:22–4:1; and Eph. 6:5–9). Paul sent Onesimus back to Philemon (see below), even while encouraging other enslaved Christians to secure their freedom if the opportunity presented itself (cf. 1 Cor. 7:21–22). Even Jesus told numerous parables commonly assuming the presence of slaves and masters (e.g., Matt. 13:24–30; 18:22–34 and Luke 12:35–40; 14:16–24): "Who among you would say to your slave who has just come in from plowing or tending sheep in the field, 'Come here at once and take your place at the table'? Would you not rather say to him, 'Prepare supper for me, put on your apron and serve me while I eat and drink; later you may eat and drink'? Do you thank the slave for doing what was commanded?" (Luke 17:7–9).

In the centuries to follow, few Christians would challenge the phenomenon of people enslaving other people as a common part of the social order. Eventually, the European World, which had instigated the Transatlantic Slave Trade, opposed human bondage. Finally, effective outcries for change appeared in the United States only in the decades leading up to the Civil War. But, for the most part, the Bible "stood" on the side of human bondage.

A short, common summary of the biblical argument went as follows. The patriarchs of ancient Israel assumed the practice; God's law required the practice; Jesus chose not to condemn the practice; early Christian churches sustained the practice. Among nineteenth-century advocates for human bondage, it was widely held that God placed special favor upon some of the greatest slaveholders of ancient Israel. With these accounts, pro-slavery advocates made a significant point.

When supporters of the U.S. bondage system turned their attention to the New Testament, they underlined Jesus's silence on the topic to conclude that the founder of Christianity himself recognized the lawfulness of the institution in its Greco-Roman form. Along with his use of the "slave" as a model of the disciple, Jesus's relative silence consented to the participation of slaveholders in the house churches, without condemnation: "a disciple is not above the teacher, nor a slave above the master" (Matt. 10:24). Many advocates, unsurprisingly, emphasized the Pauline command of "slaves obey your masters" as codes for good conduct in these Christian gatherings and clear evidence for the compatibility of Christianity with slavery (Glancy 2002). With such explicit provisions in both testaments, the pro-slavery argument based on the Bible was on a firm literary and religious foundation.

Paul's thoughts on slavery: 1 Corinthians 7:20–24 and Philemon

There are many biblical passages that support human bondage in the ancient world. There are few, if any, that oppose the institutional practice outright. Let's take a brief look at a few letters from the so-called apostle of freedom, Paul. The great sociologist, Orlando Patterson, in his extensive study on *Freedom in the Making of Western Culture*, would claim the following about Paul's social context: "The fact that people considered freedom the most important thing in life is in no way inconsistent with a tolerance for the institution of slavery ..." (Patterson 1991, 321). Apparently, for first-century Christians, the early baptismal formula—"there is no longer slave or free" (Gal. 3:28)—did not necessarily mean that entrance into the community of believers automatically altered the status of the enslaved. Rather, what Paul regularly taught in most churches was to remain in the position in life in which one initially became a believer (1 Cor. 7:17–24), whether circumcised or not (1 Cor. 7:18–19), enslaved or free (1 Cor. 7:21–23), married or single (1 Cor. 7:27). Of course, Paul's notions about the end of the world may provide a crucial backdrop for his thinking and advice: "For the present form of this world is passing away" (1 Cor. 7:31). So, why change?

Yet, at the same time, Paul could also encourage enslaved believers to secure their freedom if an occasion presented itself (1 Cor. 7:21). The New Revised Standard Version (NRSV) of the

Bible translates the Greek, which it assumes are Paul's words, like this: "Were you a slave when called? Do not be concerned about it. Even if you can gain your freedom, *make use of your present condition now* more than ever" (1 Cor. 7:21, NRSV). However, most biblical scholars suggest the Revised Standard Version (RSV) has the more original meaning (Harrill 2009): "Were you a slave when called? Never mind. But if you can gain your freedom, avail yourself of the opportunity" (1 Cor. 7:21, RSV). This guidance would also coincide well with Paul's advice to those who are "free" not to sell themselves into debt slavery: "You were bought with a price; do not become slaves of human masters" (1 Cor. 7:23, NRSV). Paul must have understood the incredible dilemma that enslaved believers would face if they served masters who were less obliging of their newfound religious status.

Paul's letter to Philemon may provide an example of one situation in which Paul had an opportunity to put actions behind the words in 1 Corinthians 7:21. This letter was not a treatise on the Roman institution of human bondage, but it addressed the specific situation of one enslaved believer, Onesimus, and his Christian slaveholder, Philemon. Paul was a social conservative with radical religious ideas. As E. P. Sanders would put it, "Paul's radical theology...could potentially have very profound social results, but prior to the [endtime] he did not want his churches to disturb the social order" (Sanders 2015, 696; author's emphasis). That also seemed to be the case in Onesimus's situation.

Paul self-identified as an apostle to the Gentiles. As an active missionary, Paul traveled to numerous cities north of the Mediterranean Sea, preached his gospel message, and planted Christian house-churches for people who believed his message. Then he departed for the next major city to begin the process all over again. When conflicts arose in these churches, Paul would visit the congregation, send one of his assistants, or write a letter in an attempt to manage the situation.

One letter that is distinct from others was Paul's letter to "Philemon." Addressing the entire household church (Phlm. 1:1–2), Paul discussed the upcoming return of Onesimus, a person who was assisting Paul at the time of the letter but who was also enslaved by Philemon. Apparently, it was time for Onesimus to return to Philemon's house. Paul expressed concern that Onesimus be treated fairly when he returned, accepted "as a beloved brother" (Phlm.

1:16). It is unclear how Onesimus came to Paul's assistance in the first place. Was he sent by the local church to help and care for Paul during Paul's imprisonment? Or, did Onesimus escape a difficult situation, seeking Paul's support in a conflict with his master, Philemon? The letter did not reveal the reason. What is clear was that Paul sent him back to the household church community and to his slave-master! What is also clear was that Paul desired for Onesimus to be treated in the way Paul himself would be treated by Philemon: "receive him as you would receive me" (Phlm. 1:17). Near the end of the letter, Paul threatened to review the situation on his trip to town (Phlm. 1:22). It is unknown whether Paul was able to make the trip.

Slavery was, in fact, an ancient Israelite practice that continued in Jewish communities into the Greco-Roman period (Hezser 2006). The public reading of the sacred writings in Jewish synagogues may not have challenged the Roman law on slavery directly. But there was one significant difference in Jewish law that is potentially relevant to Paul's letter. According to Deuteronomy 23:15, an escaped slave should *not* be returned to his master. As mentioned above, most biblical scholars assume that this regulation referred only to non-Israelite escapees. Philo (20–54 C.E.), a learned Jewish contemporary of Paul, interpreted Deuteronomy 23 as if the fugitive should not be returned to a *cruel* master, indicating that the person could be sold to someone else for his safety (*On the Virtues* XXIV.124). Furthermore, unlike most contemporary biblical scholars, Philo thought that the fugitive referred to an Israelite. Paul desired to send Onesimus back to Philemon's household with hopes that Philemon would view Onesimus through a different lens: "[N]o longer as a slave but more than a slave, a beloved brother... both in the flesh and in the Lord" (Phlm. 1:16). Paul utilized very skillful rhetoric in an attempt to convince Philemon of the justice of his cause.

After a traditional opening, Paul praised Philemon for his "love for the saints," an expression of encouragement to Paul and his mission. Then, the apostle turned to the central issue at hand (Phlm. 1:10–13). Significantly, Paul appropriated language usually reserved for family members in order to introduce Onesimus. The Greek word order is crucial: "I appeal to you on behalf of my child, whom I have birthed during my imprisonment, Onesimus" (my translation). Paul's feminine imagery of "giving birth" (*gennaō*) to

Onesimus expressed *motherly* sensibilities, which are unfortunately lost in the NRSV translation: "whose father I have become" (v. 10). Paul applied this pregnancy term to his relationship with Corinthian believers elsewhere (1 Cor. 4:15), though he usually reserved the verb to describe women like Rebecca (Rom. 9:11), Hagar, and Sarah (Gal. 4:23–24). Perhaps this was a subtle appeal to secure the support of the prominent female leader in the Christian church, "sister Apphia" (Phlm. 1:2). Furthermore, the "birth" suggests a new beginning for Onesimus, leading some scholars to conclude that this refers to Onesimus's conversion under Paul's tutelage.

The language of Philemon 1:11 has also raised much intrigue among interpreters. It states that Onesimus has become "useful" to Paul, but what does this mean? There are few hints in this brief one-sided correspondence, but his usefulness was connected to the service Onesimus provided Paul during his imprisonment (Phlm. 1:13). Was Onesimus sent to Paul by the church community in the same manner as someone named Epaphroditus (Phil. 2:25–30)? Was Philemon actually loaning Onesimus—and his service as a slave—to Paul? This possibility would call into question the fugitive theory widely held in biblical scholarship (Callahan 1997).

Philemon 1:18 provided a hint that Onesimus may have committed some egregious wrong: "If he has wronged you in any way or owes you anything, charge that to my account" (NRSV). The "reality" may not be what Paul perceived, but interpreters only have access to Paul's words. Was it Onesimus's absence from Philemon's household that has caused him economic loss? If Onesimus actually stole something from Philemon, which the passage does *not* explicitly say, it may have been additional funds to secure adequate food for his travel to Paul! In any case, Paul requested that the charges be applied to his own account. Paul desired to keep the record straight and may also have wanted to offer payment for the service he received from Onesimus. More significantly, Paul did not request forgiveness for Onesimus's actions, but promises reparations. So, against the dictates of the Torah (cf. Deut. 23:15)—if Onesimus was indeed a fugitive—but in line with Roman mores, Paul dispatched Onesimus back to the house church in Colossae.

Despite the implications of Philemon 1:18, Paul still desired for a safe return for Onesimus: Philemon should accept Onesimus back "no longer as a slave but more than a slave, a beloved brother" (Phlm. 1:15–16). Was Paul asking for Onesimus's freedom? Or, should Philemon accept Onesimus back without any legal penalty (including the possible penalty of death), allowing him to return to his former responsibilities? From our perspective in a Western democracy in which the concept of freedom is central to our national identity, the meaning of Paul's words in Philemon 1:16 will determine how we interpret the remainder of Paul's thoughts. In this setting, what would "brother" mean?

May Paul's use of "brother" for Onesimus (Phlm. 1:20) indicate both a spiritual and social status? In Paul's egalitarian words, Onesimus should be considered a brother "in the Lord" *and* "in the flesh" (Phlm. 1:16). This last phrase attempted to allude to the human relationship between Onesimus and Philemon. When Paul used this phrase elsewhere, he generally referred to a person's physical condition (cf. Rom. 2:28; 2 Cor. 10:3; Gal. 2:20; and Phil. 1:22). Can Philemon treat Onesimus as a "brother...in the flesh" without altering their own social relationship? Is Paul simply encouraging Philemon to consider Onesimus his brother-slave, that is, a "brother" spiritually, but a "slave" socially?

Approaching the end of his letter, Paul adds a personal touch, by announcing his upcoming plans to visit the Phrygian household church (Phlm. 1:22). The potential weight of such rhetoric cannot be overstated in this ancient setting. Whether Paul actually intended to visit, his announcement lent seriousness to Philemon's decision. One way or another, Paul would learn of Philemon's actions through the missionary grapevine. Even if Paul was unable to travel to this community, Paul had numerous associates working in the nascent missionary movement who could potentially make a visit in lieu of the apostle. As with the endings of other letters, Paul sent greetings from "fellow workers" before closing with a final blessing (Phlm. 1:25). The need for "grace" (*charis*) was absolutely necessary in the situation at hand.

Whatever interpreters may think about this short but poignant letter, one fact remains. Paul was *not* indifferent to Onesimus's plight. He utilizes his vast rhetorical skill to secure an altered condition for his fellow believer in Christ. Perhaps Paul viewed the situation as an example of what he wrote to enslaved Corinthian believers: "But if you can gain your freedom, avail yourself of the opportunity" (1 Cor. 7:21, RSV). Yet, Paul remains an ambiguous witness to freedom. Why Paul returned Onesimus at all remains unanswerable. His appeal to "love" among Christians may be one reason. He didn't want to force the Christian slave owner's hand into freeing his Christian slave.

We are also left wondering how Onesimus felt about Paul's decision. The letter does not seem to provide any clues into the thoughts of this enslaved believer, even though many readers might wish to identify as much with Onesimus as they would with Paul or Philemon. Identifying with the enslaved, some may have hoped for a more forceful argument.

The ambiguity of Paul's request, and the circumstances surrounding this situation, has led to misunderstanding and misuse of this document in the history of its interpretation. Some of Paul's earliest followers—including the writers of Ephesians, Colossians, Timothy, and Titus—would have no problem envisioning prominent roles for slaveholders in the early house churches (cf. Eph. 6; Col. 3–4; 1 Tim. 6; and Titus 2). This would be a "natural" outgrowth of Paul's more socially conservative stance on issues surrounding slavery and, perhaps, the ambiguous nature of Paul's request in this letter (Martin 2010).

In another time and place, African-Americans, unfortunately, have borne the brunt of (mis)interpretations of Paul's position from nineteenth-century antebellum pro-slavery corners in the United States. These New Testament texts may have supported human bondage, but not the kind that included racial distinctions in the U.S. version of enslavement practices. Paul's expectations were high that Philemon would do "even more" than asked. Some scholars imagine that Paul's request for Onesimus's release was of a limited kind, one that would bind Onesimus to Paul's mission, as Paul's "slave" to assist him in the spread of the Gospel.

There are many gaps in the letters of the New Testament that complicate interpretation. As one who was now a "Christian" and a "slave," what would Onesimus have imagined the next time he heard the early Christian baptismal formula?

As many of you as were baptized into Christ have clothed yourselves with Christ. There is no longer Jew or Greek, there is no longer slave or free, there is no longer male and female; for all of you are one in Christ Jesus. (Gal. 3:27–28)

Final reflections:
The Bible can't speak for itself!

It is important to acknowledge that the Bible cannot speak for itself. Careful, critical interpretations may allow us to understand biblical passages in their ancient cultural settings. But contemporary scholars also bring their own biases into these interpretive exercises. It is much easier to see examples of these prejudices in an earlier historical time, such as during the period surrounding the passage of the Fugitive Slave Act of 1850. It is much more difficult to recognize our own twenty-first-century interpretative biases as we engage the contemporary issues of our day. What cannot be stressed enough is to remember that the Bible cannot take a side in moral issues. As a collection of ancient documents of mixed genres, it should not be expected to provide solutions for complex contemporary concerns in a post-Enlightenment world.

I am not suggesting that contemporary people stop reading the Bible. However, I am asserting that we should proceed with a basic understanding of the complexity of interpretation. This includes a fundamental awareness that it is common for people of good will—on both sides of an issue—to find (selective) support for their position from the pages of the Bible. This does not mean that one should claim "the Bible is on my side." The Bible could not resolve the slavery debate of the nineteenth-century generation; it took a civil war! The Bible cannot choose sides; interpreters do. The Bible cannot speak for itself. It will always need contemporary translators, and those interpreters are influenced by more ideological concerns than those the Bible presents.

Works Cited

Basler, Roy P. (ed.). *Abraham Lincoln: His Speeches and Writings*. New York: De Capo, 1946.

Callahan, Allen. *Embassy of Onesimus: The Letter of Paul to Philemon*. Bloomsbury: T&T Clark, 1997.

Coates, Ta-Nehisi. "Why Precisely Is Bernie Sanders against Reparations?" *The Atlantic*. January 19, 2016. http://www.theatlantic.com/politics/archive/2016/01/bernie-sanders-reparations/424602/ (accessed March 1, 2016).

Franklin, John Hope. *Reconstruction after the Civil War*, 2nd edn. Chicago, IL: University of Chicago Press, 1994.

Glancy, Jennifer. *Slavery in Early Christianity*. Oxford: Oxford University Press, 2002.

Harrill, J. Albert. "Slavery." In *The New Interpreter's Dictionary of the Bible*, edited by Katharine Doob Sakenfeld. Vol. 5, 299–308. Nashville, TN: Abingdon, 2009.

Hezser, Catherine. *Jewish Slavery in Antiquity*. Oxford and New York: Oxford University Press, 2006.

Martin, Clarice. "The Eyes Have It: Slaves in the Communities of Christ Believers." In *The People's History: Christian Origins*, edited by Richard Horsley, 221–239. Minneapolis, MN: Fortress Press, 2010.

Paterson, Orlando. *Freedom: Volume I: Freedom in the Making of Western Culture*. New York, NY: Basic Books, 1991.

Powery, Emerson. "Letter to Philemon." In *New Interpreter's One-Volume Commentary on the Bible*, edited by David L. Peterson and Beverly Roberts Gaventa, 877–880. Nashville, TN: Abingdon, 2010.

Sanders, E.P. *Paul: The Apostle's Life, Letters, and Thought*. Minneapolis, MN: Fortress Press, 2015.

Scott, Eugene. "Sanders Campaign Defends Opposition to Slavery Reparations." *CNN*. January 21, 2016. http://www.cnn.com/2016/01/21/politics/bernie-sanders-slavery-reparations/ (accessed January 22, 2016).

Stuart, Moses. *Conscience and Constitution*. Boston, MA: Crocker & Brewster, 1850.

Tigay, Jeffrey. *Deuteronomy*. The Jewish Publication Society Torah Commentary Series. Jerusalem: JPS, 1996.

Vavreck, Lynn. "Measuring Donald Trump's Supporters for Intolerance." *New York Times*. February 23, 2016. http://www.nytimes.com/2016/02/25/upshot/measuring-donald-trumps-supporters-for-intolerance.html (accessed February 25, 2016).

YouGov Poll. *The Economist*. January 15–19, 2016. https://d25d2506sfb94s.cloudfront.net/cumulus_uploads/document/ctucuikdsj/econToplines.pdf (accessed February 8, 2016).

Zurcher, Anthony. "Ben Carson Compares Abortion to Slavery." *BBC*. October 26, 2015. http://www.bbc.com/news/world-us-canada-34641563 (accessed March 1, 2016).

11

Women, the Bible, and the Nineteenth Amendment to the U.S. Constitution

Christopher A. Rollston

Aspects of women's suffrage in the late nineteenth and early twentieth centuries in the United States

The bloodshed of World War I had finally ceased, Henry Ford's Model T was rolling off Detroit's "moving assembly lines" at an astonishing pace, President Woodrow Wilson was recovering from a stroke, Prohibition was the law of the land, and a young man named Al Capone had just moved to Chicago. Moreover, and at long last, an amendment that guaranteed women the right to vote had become part of the U.S. Constitution. The year was 1920. The Nineteenth Amendment reads as follows: "The right of citizens of the United States to vote shall not be denied or abridged by the United States or by any State on account of sex. Congress shall have power to enforce this article by appropriate legislation."

The battle for the ballot box had been bitter, personal, divisive, iterative, and long. Some seventy years prior to the ratification of the Nineteenth Amendment, Elizabeth Cady Stanton (1815–1902) and Lucretia Coffin Mott (1793–1880) had been two of the primary organizers of the famed Seneca Falls Convention of 1848, the first women's rights convention in the United States. It was at that meeting that Elizabeth Stanton presented her famed *Declaration of Sentiments*, and this declaration was signed by some 100 women and men in attendance, including Charlotte Woodward, Rhoda Palmer, James Mott, and Frederick Douglas. Modeled on the U.S. Declaration of Independence, among the opening words of the preamble of the *Declaration of Sentiments* are these:

> When, in the course of human events, it becomes necessary for one portion of the family of man to assume among the people of the earth a position different from that which they have hitherto occupied, but one to which the laws of nature and of nature's God entitle them, a decent respect to the opinions of mankind requires that they should declare the causes that impel them to such a course. We hold these truths to be self-evident: that all men and women are created equal; that they are endowed by their Creator with certain inalienable rights; that among these are life, liberty, and the pursuit of happiness.

The Preamble of the *Declaration of Sentiments* concludes with these words:

> The history of mankind is a history of repeated injuries and usurpation on the part of man toward woman, having in direct object the establishment of an absolute tyranny over her. To prove this, let facts be submitted to a candid world.

At that juncture, the *Declaration of Sentiments* enumerates some of the facets of society's marginalization of women, something that was occurring under the leadership and auspices of a male-dominated American society. Here is a selection of some of the grievances.

> He deprived her of this first right as a citizen, the elective franchise, thereby leaving her without representation in the halls of legislation, he has oppressed her on all sides.
>   In the covenant of marriage, she is compelled to promise obedience to her husband, he becoming, to all intents and

purposes, her master—the law giving him power to deprive her of her liberty, and to administer chastisement.

He closes against her all the avenues to wealth and distinction, which he considers most honorable to himself. As a teacher of theology, medicine, or law, she is not known.

He has denied her the facilities for obtaining a thorough education—all colleges being closed against her.

Now, in view of this entire disfranchisement of one-half the people of this country, their social and religious degradation.... we insist that women have immediate admission to all the rights and privileges which belong to them as citizens of the United States. (Stanton 1889, 70–71)

Some three years after the Seneca Falls Convention, Elizabeth Stanton met Susan B. Anthony (1820–1906) and together they (among many others) labored persistently for women's suffrage.

Often in public discourse about the ballot box during this era, the content of the Bible was front and center. Of course, formal public debates about politics and religion were also particularly common during the nineteenth century and the early twentieth century. In October 1882, a spirited debate in which the Bible became central occurred between a newspaper editor (of the Omaha Bee) named Edward Rosewater and Susan B. Anthony. During the course of the debate, before an immense crowd, Susan B. Anthony said: "All men...have conspired together to make the laws and do the governing of the nation, and to rule over us without our consent.... This is a grand monopoly on the part of the men." Edward Rosewater (an avowed anti-suffragist) then retorted: "*That monopoly was created by a higher power. It is a monopoly created by the Lord*" (Gordon et al. 2006, 188; cf. Gordon 2012, 201–233, esp. 206, emphasis mine). Rosewater was attempting to trump Anthony's arguments by appealing to the putative words of God himself, the Bible.

Susan B. Anthony's close friend Elizabeth Cady Stanton knew the Bible masterfully well and Stanton was conversant with the best of the biblical scholarship of the time (including historical criticism). She heartily picked up the gauntlet. Stanton assembled an impressive array of scholars of the Bible, all of whom were women, and a *magnum opus* entitled *The Woman's Bible* soon appeared. Stanton was the general editor (Stanton 1895, 1898). This was a watershed moment in the history of biblical studies. After all, Stanton was among the first to discern (and to state in a published volume), that the Bible, as important as it is in human history, often had a discernible male bias.

Biblical literacy: Well... yes and no

During the course of teaching the Bible for several decades in churches, synagogues, confessional institutions of higher education, and non-confessional institutions of higher education, I have discerned that people often assume that they know the contents of the biblical text rather well. In reality, sometimes this is the case and sometimes this is not. That is, most people will know certain components of the Bible fairly well, but with some blocks of material they will have passing familiarity at best. For example, many will know that Abraham had sons with Sarah and Hagar, but few will know the name of the woman whom Abraham married after Sarah's death, a woman with whom he had six sons, *all of whom are named in the text* (Gen. 25:2–6). Similarly, many people know the major stories about King David, but few can name the centuries during which King Jehu or King Hoshea reigned, nor the major events surrounding them, though these are nicely recorded in Second Kings (2 Kgs. 9–10 and 17). The case is similar for the New Testament, although it is a much smaller corpus of literature. I have found that some people will know (certain) portions of the gospels, but a relatively small number of people know which two gospels contain nativity accounts and are also able to discuss the details of the dramatic differences between these accounts (Matt. 1:18–21 and Luke 2:1–38). Similarly, it is a relatively small number who can name the name of the apostle who replaced Judas Iscariot (Acts 1:15–26), or the content of the Book of Jude. This list could go on and on. In sum, for the Hebrew Bible and for the New Testament, some of the biblical content is well known, but there is modest familiarity with many of the major and minor details of the Bible. That is fine, of course, but it does mean that people will often be surprised at the actual content of the biblical text. Such is often the case as well with the Bible's material about women.

Women in the Bible:
Candor about content

The lens of a historian and linguist is sometimes different from the lens of a member of a church or synagogue. After all, it is fairly commonplace for a priest, pastor, or rabbi to find biblical texts that are encouraging and useful in building a foundation of morality and justice. This is important and good. Congregants and parishioners are often very grateful for this. With these sorts of intentions in place, however, there is sometimes a natural desire to avoid problem texts, the disconcerting texts, and the disheartening perspectives of some of the authors of biblical texts. I also understand that desire and, I suppose that during my life, I have sometimes avoided certain texts in preparing my own lessons, lectures, and homilies. But a decade or two ago, I decided that this could cause those hearing my words to have a partial, laundered, or even naïve view of Scripture. Ultimately, therefore, I decided that it was the entire Scripture that I would focus on in my teaching and writing, not just the texts that my listeners would find wholesome and morally and religiously acceptable. That is, I want to be honest about biblical content.

So let me focus on some of the difficult facets of the Bible, the patriarchal lenses of some of its authors, and the ways in which some of these authors viewed women as lesser. The "texts of terror" (e.g., rape, incest, and forced marriages to conquerors) such as those that have been so capably discussed by colleagues such as Phyllis Trible (1984) and Phyllis Bird (1997), I shall leave for another occasion. In this chapter, I'm particularly interested in the worldviews and perspectives of the authors, and sadly this is a framework that often marginalizes women. But at the conclusion of this chapter, I shall look at several biblical texts that push back against some of these troubling texts, that is, some particularly redemptive materials in this broad corpus of the Bible.

The great narratives of Genesis are among those that are best known within both Judaism and Christianity, stories about creation, the flood, and stories about Abraham and Sarah, Isaac and Rebekah, and Jacob and Rachel and Leah. Rightfully so. But let's probe more deeply into some of these famous narratives of Genesis, attempting to see things that we may, or may not, have noticed. Adam and Eve had three sons: Cain, Abel, and Seth. Yes, this is the testimony of the Bible, but these are just *some of* the children of Adam and Eve. For Scripture states that "Adam fathered (Hebrew: *wayyôled*) sons and daughters" after the birth of Seth (Gen. 5:4). So we know the names of three of the sons of Adam and Eve, but the Bible does not provide the name of even one of their daughters. Similarly, the Scripture notes that "Noah fathered Shem, Ham, and Japheth" (Gen. 5:32). But the Bible does not provide the name of their mother, nor does it provide the names of the wives of his sons. All eight were on Noah's ark and all departed from the ark after the great flood (Gen. 8:18 and 1 Pet. 3:20). *We know the names of all the men, but none of the women.*

In the case of the Patriarch Jacob, the names of his wives are known, Rachel and Leah, and we know the names of the maidservants of his wives with whom he also had children, Bilhah and Zilpah. Furthermore, we know the names of all twelve of his sons, Reuben, Simeon, Levi, Judah, Issachar, Zebulun, Dan, Naphtali, Gad, Asher, Joseph, and Benjamin (Gen. 29:31–30:24; 35:16–21). It's a long list. But the Bible states that Jacob had sons *and daughters*. For example, after Joseph is sold into slavery by his brothers, the text states: "All Jacob's sons and daughters arose to comfort him, but he refused to be comforted" (Gen. 37:35). And after Jacob learned that Joseph was alive and well and thriving in Egypt, the text states: "And Jacob brought with him to Egypt: his sons, and the sons of his sons, and his daughters, and the daughters of his sons, and all his seed" (Gen. 46:7). But, of course, the names of his daughters are not given in the Bible, with the exception of his daughter Dinah, since she was raped. Because this is recounted in detail in the Bible (Gen. 34), we know her name.

Some might attempt to justify this preponderance of the names of the men and the dearth of the names of the women. For example, someone might suggest that part of the reason for the omission of the names of daughters was that the family land (the paternal estate, in Hebrew *naḥalah*) belonged to the sons, not the daughters. The inheritance customs in place were certainly part of the reason for the emphasis on the names of sons and fathers, but the fact remains that the names of so many daughters are lost forever, never to be remembered or recited. Not then, not now. I hope that we can all grieve the fact that we don't have these names. We are the poorer for not having them.

Let's look further, this time at some legal material. The Ten Commandments are quite well known. It is often stated (quite accurately) that the first four commandments revolve around the intended audience's relationship with God (e.g., the worship of Yahweh alone, no graven images, no vain usage of the divine name, and remembrance of the Sabbath day), and that the final six commandments revolve around proper social conduct (e.g., honoring parents, not murdering, not stealing, not committing adultery, and not committing perjury). Now let's look at the intended audience, especially the gender of the intended audience. The content of the tenth commandment is the most revealing in this regard: "You shall not covet your neighbor's house, you shall not covet your neighbor's wife, or his male slave, his female slave, his ox, his donkey or anything which belongs to your neighbor" (Exod. 20:17 and Deut. 5:21).

Because the Ten Commandments are so well known, it's quite easy to miss the assumptions in them about gender. But the marginalization of women is clear. The wife is classified as her husband's property and she's listed with the slaves and work animals. There's also a striking omission in this commandment: never does it say "You shall not covet your neighbor's husband." The Ten Commandments were written to men, not women.

I'm certainly not the first to notice or mention this. In fact, Elizabeth Cady Stanton emphasized this long, long ago. Here is her voice on the matter: "Suppose we reverse the language and see how one-sided it would seem addressed only to women...'Thou shalt not covet thy neighbor's husband, nor her field, nor her ox, nor anything that is thy neighbor's'" (Stanton 1895, 126).

There is even linguistic evidence regarding gender bias in the Ten Commandments. Hebrew has four distinct forms of the word "you" and these are gender and number specific. The form of "you" in every single commandment is masculine singular. The text assumes its readers are men. True, mothers are mentioned in the Decalogue as deserving of honor, but even here the Hebrew grammar assumes a male readership: the Hebrew verb for "honor" is masculine singular (Exod. 20:12 and Deut. 5:16). This prompted a prominent female scholar to write an article about the Ten Commandments entitled "The Decalogue—Am I an Addressee?" (Brenner 1994, 255–258). The question in the title of Brenner's article is a fair one, based on the content of the laws and even the Hebrew grammar itself. Ultimately, the Ten Commandments embody much that is foundational for modern society, but they are not egalitarian: they assume an exclusively male audience.

Additional legal texts further reveal the marginalized status of women. For example, an unmarried woman could be compelled to marry her rapist, as long as the rapist could pay the standard bride price and the woman's father was comfortable with the marriage (Deut. 22:28–29 and Exodus 22:16–17). And some fathers were comfortable, if Jacob is any indication (Gen. 34). Polygyny (a man having multiple wives at the same time) was not condemned, but was an accepted and legal custom (Deut. 21:15–17; Gen. 4:19–24; and 2 Sam. 3:2–5). A woman's religious vow could be nullified by her father or her husband (Num. 30:3–15). And the assumption of the text is that the priesthood is all male (Lev. 21). In short, within the legal literature of the Bible, women were not accorded the same status as men.

Women are marginalized in biblical wisdom literature as well, including the Book of Proverbs. For example, quite a number of times Proverbs uses the phrase "my son" (e.g., Prov. 1:8, 10; 2:1; 3:1; 4:10; 5:1), but the phrase "my daughter" does not occur. The commands in Proverbs are consistently second-person masculine, never second-person feminine. The readership of the Book of Proverbs is warned to beware of the evil seductress (e.g., Prov. 5), but the reverse doesn't occur: never does the book warn women to beware of a male seducer. The authors say living with a contentious woman is terrible, but never say the same about a contentious man (Prov. 25:24). True, there is a famous text in Proverbs which praises a "noble wife" (Prov. 31:10–31). She is wise, benevolent, hardworking, an entrepreneur, and loved by her sons and husband (daughters are not mentioned). Readers are encouraged to find such a wife. But there is a subtle problem: there is no counterpart to the "noble wife" text—nothing in the book that encourages young women to find a noble husband. After all, men were the intended readers, not women.

The New Testament contains texts that marginalize women as well. Among the harshest of these texts is 1 Timothy 2. The author is discussing worship and begins by stating that "men should pray" (and the word used here for men is *andras*, a gendered word that refers only to males) and then says "women should dress themselves modestly and decently" (vv. 8–9). So men are to pray and women are to dress modestly. That's quite a contrast. But there's more: "Let a woman learn in silence and full submission. I permit no woman to teach or to have authority over a man; she is to be silent" (vv. 11–12). The author's rationale: "For Adam was formed first, then Eve, and Adam was not deceived, but the woman was deceived and became a transgressor" (vv. 13–14). According to this text, women were to be silent in worship gatherings (and men were certainly not told to be silent), and the rationale for this mandate is that woman (Eve) was created second and sinned first. And the final blow is this: a woman "will be saved" (the future tense of the standard word for "be saved," "be given salvation") through childbirth, if she remains in faith and love and sanctification with modesty" (1 Tim. 2:15). In Part 2 of Elizabeth Cady Stanton's *The Woman's Bible*, Lucinda B. Chandler penned these words about 1 Timothy 2: "But that...woman should have been condemned and punished for trying to get knowledge, and forbidden to impart what she has learned, is the most unaccountable peculiarity of masculine wisdom" (Stanton 1898, 163). Chandler certainly has a point, and she made it more than a century ago.

I have heard some people attempt to soften these texts from 1 Timothy 2 and to suggest that "we are all supposed to learn in submission, men and women." The difficulty with that line of interpretation is that the text is definitively delineating gender roles in the church and at the end of the day, *this text declares that women are to be silent and dress modestly and men are to pray.* The men are not told to be silent. Also, I have heard some attempt to soften the patriarchy of this text by suggesting that there were some "problem women" creating trouble in ecclesiastical circles in Ephesus, and so this was a localized problem at Ephesus. The difficulty with that line of interpretation is that *no such "problem women" are mentioned in this section of the text*, while some *"problem men"* named Alexander and Hymenaeus *are mentioned* a few verses earlier in 1 Timothy 1:20! Furthermore, *the presumed rationale for the gender-demarcated roles is explicitly mentioned in the text*: "For Adam was formed first, then Eve, and Adam was not deceived, but the woman was deceived and became a transgressor." That is, the author is not referencing a particular problem at Ephesus. He is declaring a binding, general principle that he roots in the fabric of creation itself.

Obviously, the author of 1 Timothy is marginalizing women. To suggest something different from this is to engage in *eisegesis*— what biblical scholars call an interpretation that injects our own biases into the text. Obviously, I wish that this author would not have marginalized women. I'd like some way to avoid stating that he did. But I have to be intellectually honest about the actual content of the text. Similar content is contained in the so-called Household Codes of the New Testament: husbands are commanded to "love their wives" and to avoid treating them "harshly," but women are commanded to "submit to" (Greek: *hypo-tassesthe*, literally: "be subordinate") their "husbands" (Col. 3:18–19 and Eph. 5:22–25).

Fortunately, there were some biblical authors who felt differently, authors who pushed back against the standard ancient practice of marginalizing women. The author of Job is my favorite. According to the Bible, Job had seven sons and three daughters. Of course, according to standard practice, the sons would always receive the ancestral land (*nahalah*), while the daughters would normally receive a dowry, worth much less. Daughters could only receive the ancestral land *when there were no sons*, something the case of the daughters of Zelophehad demonstrates (Num. 27:1–11). Since Job had sons—seven of them—standard legal custom would dictate that the ancestral estate would be divided among them. Furthermore, as I have noted, biblical authors will often give us the names of sons but not daughters.

However, the author of the Book of Job was an iconoclast and he was progressive. Thus, throughout the entire book, Job's author is critiquing traditional concepts of theodicy—the question of why bad things happen to people. Once he had finished that critique, he takes one final swipe, this time at patriarchal customs. Here is his book's grand conclusion:

> Job had seven sons and three daughters. And he named the first one Jemimah, and the second Keziah, and the third Keren-Happuch. And no women as beautiful as the daughters of Job could be found in all the land. And their father gave to them a *nahalah* along with their brothers. And after this Job lived one

hundred and forty years and he saw his sons, and the sons of his sons to the fourth generation. And Job died an old man, full of days. (Job 42:13–17)

So with his final words, Job's author turned conventional legal practice and naming practices on their heads: *he names all the daughters, but none of the sons, and he states that Job gave his daughters a naḥalah, even though Job had sons.* I always envision the author of Job smiling broadly as he, or she, placed the reed pen down upon the completed papyrus manuscript.

In addition, I am always pleased to emphasize that the author of Judges describes Deborah as a prophetess (*nevi'ah*), a judge, and a warrior (Jud. 4–5). And the author of Kings describes Huldah as a prophetess (*nevi'ah*) capable of understanding the book of the law that was discovered in the Jerusalem Temple, even though the highest officials in the land were not able to do so (2 Kgs. 22:14–20). The authors of the books of Ruth and Esther also portray the women in their books as strong, though Naomi, Ruth, and Esther still had to labor under, and live within, patriarchal social structures.

Similarly, within the New Testament, there are texts and authors who pushed back against patriarchy. For example, there is reference to Annah (Hannah) as a prophetess (*profētis*) in the Jerusalem Temple (Luke 2:36–38). The author of Acts refers to the daughters of Deacon Philip as having four daughters with the gift of prophecy (Acts 21:9). Furthermore, the Apostle Paul states that there is "no longer Jew nor Greek, slave nor free, male nor female" (Gal. 3:28). He also refers to "Phoebe our sister who is a deacon (Greek: *diakonos*) of the Church" (Rom. 16:1) and to Junia as "preeminent among the apostles" (Rom. 16:7). Paul also assumed that it was permissible for women to prophesy (1 Cor. 11:5).

I wish that I could always focus on those biblical texts that reflect a high view of women. I wish I could say that all the authors of the Bible had a high view of women and that none marginalized women. But I am a historian and linguist, and so I must anchor my views in the total evidence, not just the evidence that I like the most. Women were often devalued in the ancient Near Eastern and Mediterranean worlds, with a fair number of the biblical authors participating. But, though not great in number, there were some precious voices among the biblical authors who pushed back against the marginalization of daughters, mothers, wives, aunts, sisters, and grandmothers. I wish to foreground those voices, to applaud those brave and progressive biblical authors. I hope that this is your wish as well.

Acknowledgments

I am very grateful to Rodney Werline and Frances Flannery for requesting that I write a chapter for this volume. Moreover, I am also grateful to my research assistants Danielle Weeks, Grace Delaney, and Talya Steinberg for bibliographic assistance with this article. I dedicate this chapter to my mother and my father, both of whom always model gender equality in the public and the private spheres of life. I shall always be in their debt.

Works Cited

Bird, Phyllis A. *Missing Persons and Mistaken Identities: Women and Gender in Ancient Israel*. Overtures to Biblical Theology Series. Minneapolis: Fortress Press, 1997.

Brenner, Athalya. "An Afterword: The Decalogue—Am I an Addressee?" In *A Feminist Companion to Exodus to Deuteronomy*, edited by Athalya Brenner, 255–258. The Feminist Companion to the Bible 6: Sheffield: Sheffield Academic Press, 1994.

Gordon, Ann D. "Knowing Susan B. Anthony: The Stories We Tell of a Life" In *Susan B. Anthony and the Struggle for Equal Rights: Volume 4*, edited by Christine L. Ridarsky and Mary M. Huth, 201-234. Rochester: University of Rochester Press, 2012.

Gordon, Ann D., Frazier, Krystal, Doig, Lesley L., Westkaemper, Emily and Chapdelaine, Robin (eds.). *The Selected Papers of Elizabeth Cady Stanton and Susan B. Anthony: Vol. 4, When Clowns Make Laws for Queens, 1880 to 1887*. New Brunswick, NJ: Rutgers University Press, 2006.

Stanton, Elizabeth Cady. *A History of Woman Suffrage: Volume 1*. Rochester, NY: Fowler and Wells, 1889.

Stanton, Elizabeth Cady (ed.). *The Woman's Bible: Parts I and II*. New York: European Publishing Company, 1895, 1898.

Trible, Phyllis. *Texts of Terror: Literary-Feminist Readings of Biblical Narratives*. Philadelphia: Fortress Press, 1984.

PART THREE

Concluding Thoughts

12

What Is "the Bible"?

Kelley Coblentz Bautch

Introduction

The fact that the politicians and pundits cited in this volume refer to the Bible to settle policy debates shows that they assume everyone knows the authority of the Bible. How often have we heard the expression: "The Bible says…"? Typically our interest is most piqued by whatever follows: what *does* the Bible say about climate change, family values, or the role of women? But, we should also be interested in the first part of the statement: "The *Bible* says. …" What in fact *is* the Bible? How did the Bible come to be?

The Bible: Strictly defined

Sometimes people refer to the Bible as the "Good Book" and for many that is exactly what the Bible is: a singular work associated with the Divine, virtues, and morality. Technically speaking, it is more accurate to refer to the Bible as the "Good Books." The term "Bible" comes from the Greek *biblia*, a plural noun which means "documents" or "scrolls." The plural designation *biblia* is quite appropriate: what one encounters between the two covers and binding of a Bible today is a collection of documents. The reality is reflected, moreover, in titles found in English translations of the Bible like "the Book of Genesis," "the Book of Exodus," and so on.

In this regard, the Bible is an anthology, an intentional collection of texts that concern the religious traditions of ancient Near Eastern and Mediterranean lands.

Many Bibles

If you have a Bible in your home, which Bible is it? Bibles are not simply differentiated by translations like the King James Version or New International Version, but also by content. While most people likely know that the Bible used by Jews differs from the Bible used by Christians, there are diverse Bibles also for Christians. These are determined by the branch of Christianity—Orthodox, Roman Catholic, or Protestant—that claims a particular collection. While the Jewish and Christian Bibles are organized differently, even Christian Bibles differ on what to include. For instance, *The Book of Enoch* is important for many Ethiopian Orthodox Christians and included in their Bible, even though most Roman Catholics and Protestants haven't even heard of it.

Why do these Bibles differ? Simply put, there are different Bibles because there are different religious communities. Through the ages, Jews and Christians have claimed and collected ancient writings dear to them, books they understand to be inspired by God. The contents that relate to theology (beliefs about God), history, cultural context, and one's story and self-perception, though, differ according to one's community.

Consider, first, the Bible for Jewish communities. This Bible has twenty-four books and is called in traditional circles the Tanak, an acronym that refers to three sections of sacred texts (the Torah or "Instruction," the Nevi'im or "Prophets," and the Ketuvim or "Writings"). Sometimes it is called the Miqr'a, meaning "that which is recited/read." In academic circles, the Tanak or Miqr'a is often known as the Hebrew Bible, because the majority of texts in it were composed in Hebrew. This Bible begins with the story of the creation of earth and humankind (Genesis), follows the stories of famous patriarchs and monarchs, includes exhortations from prophets, as well as other writings like the Psalms, and concludes with the Jewish community's return to Israel after exile to Babylon (sixth century B.C.E.). The Tanak tells the story of Israel and God's relationship with this people.

The Bible for Christians is made up of two parts: an Old Testament and a New Testament. The Old Testament is comparable, but not identical to the Hebrew Bible or Tanak. While the latter is organized into three subsections—Torah, Prophets, and Writings—the Christian Old Testament is arranged into four sections: Pentateuch, Historical Writings, Wisdom and Poetic Writings, and Prophets. Christian and Jewish Bibles differ on what books are counted in the section called the "Prophets" and in what order those books occur. The Christian Bible begins with creation, explores Israel's history and wisdom teachings, and then includes writings of the prophets of Israel, which conclude the Old Testament. In this way, the books associated with prophets make a bridge to the writings of the New Testament, connecting Jesus to the history of Israel and connecting the Old Testament to the New Testament. This second part of the Christian Bible then takes up the life, public ministry, death and resurrection of Jesus, as well as the experiences of his first followers, from various vantages.

While all Christian Bibles share this basic structure, the contents of the Old Testament differ by communities. The Protestant Old Testament has the same subsections and arrangement as the Roman Catholic and Orthodox Old Testaments. Its contents, however, resemble the Jewish Bible, with the exception that Protestants divide the contents into thirty-nine books. The additional books found in the Roman Catholic and Orthodox Christian Old Testaments are associated with the Septuagint, the Greek translation of the Hebrew Bible used by Jews and later Christians living in Greek and Roman cultural contexts. The additional books, which are not considered "biblical" by Protestants, are often included in their Bible in a section referred to as "Apocrypha." Protestants typically situate them between the Old and New Testaments. The New Revised Standard Version, most often used in this volume, adopts this organization: Old Testament, Apocrypha, and New Testament. For this reason, the Protestant Old Testament is shorter than the Roman Catholic and Orthodox Old Testaments. As one can see, not only between Judaism and Christianity, but even among the various branches of Christianity, what we mean by "Bible" can refer to different collections and orderings of books.

How did the Bible come to be?

Typically my students will ask, "Who decided which books belong in the Bible? Why are there more books in the Roman Catholic and Orthodox Bibles than in the Protestant Bible?" The short answer is that communities (not an elite group stealing away in a smoke-filled room) decided which books to preserve and to include in their collections of writings considered authoritative. It is also clear from the historical record that these collections of religious writings (not only the compositions themselves) happened over a long period of time. That is, our Bibles are the result of complex processes. We have some general sense for how these collections developed over time, though, as any historian of antiquity would say, the evidence is not as plentiful as one would like.

The formation of the Tanak

Peoples of ancient Israel composed and passed along stories of their origins, along with tribal, royal, and religious histories (Ulrich 2010). Sayings and accounts of prophets—the spokespersons of God—as well as traditions associated with priestly rituals, hymns, and texts meant to teach "wisdom" also were part of Israel's religious literature. Most likely these traditions originated in oral settings but may have included written compositions as well (Ulrich 2010). Over time, the literature that told of the formation of Israel as a people and their relationship to God, Israel's sovereign and deliverer, coalesced as community literature. As biblical scholar Eugene Ulrich eloquently states: "Just as the community formed the literature, so too the literature formed the community as it moved through history" (Ulrich 2010, 99).

In the sixth century B.C.E., the people of Judah (the southern kingdom of what is traditionally known as Israel) suffered a devastating blow. The Babylonian Empire destroyed the central religious institution of the community, the Jerusalem Temple, and exiled the leadership and some of the population to Babylon. In the wake of this catastrophe, traditions and stories from Israel's past were braided together and these, along with fresh responses to changing situations, contributed to the growing body of

Israel's literature—the basis for the Tanak. Ulrich's explanation of the heightening status of the literature is one widely shared by scholars: "Religious leaders and pious people sincerely trying to understand and articulate the divine will produced the religious classics of Israel. As generation after generation pondered their religious traditions in light of their current historical, political and social reality, in one sense the word *about* God became the word of God" (Ulrich 2010, 101). Some of the writings of ancient Israel did claim to recite Divine speech. The prophets presented oracles of God's communication to the people with the formula "thus says the Lord" and refer to "the Word of God" (see, e.g., Jer. 22:18 and Amos 7:16). In time, authoritative writings (including even the work of narrators or selections that did not claim to be "the Word of Lord") were understood in their totality as authored by the Divine.

How do scholars know *which* "writings" were valued by early Jewish communities in the ancient world? Sadly, we don't have any elaborate discussion among Jewish scribes, priests, or community leaders preserved for us from the time before the first century C.E. to answer that question in a straightforward manner. Similarly, there is no distinct or certain list before the first century C.E. of which texts were considered authoritative for religious practice and doctrine (Lim 2013, 5). However, if we survey in general the books cited by Jews from the sixth century B.C.E. to the first century B.C.E., we do find references to works affiliated with Moses and the Torah (Neh. 8:1, 3, 8, 13 and Ezra 6:18; 7:12, 26). As collections of the Torah came together, and as collections of the various Prophets also grew, the smaller collections eventually began to circulate together.

While many of the sacred traditions that were collected were likely passed along orally, Jewish communities increasingly valued the **written** form of traditional teaching and religious history. For this reason, Jews who returned to Israel and reestablished their homeland from the late sixth century B.C.E. to late first century C.E. also cite and defer to texts called "the writings," "the writing," "the holy writing," and "the holy books" (see, e.g., Paul's letter to the Galatians 3:22). The modern day synonym for the Bible, "Scripture," comes from these designations.

It is unclear which texts were included among the Prophets. Why can't we just look in an ancient Tanak and see what texts were included in this section? Alas, we have no ancient "Bibles"—bound collections of sacred texts in fixed orders—and possess now very few biblical writings that existed prior to the first century C.E.

While most religious texts written on scrolls have not survived the ravages of time, one of the most important archaeological finds of the last century, however, was the discovery of the Dead Sea Scrolls. And these scrolls, apparently an ancient library sacred to some Jews around the second century B.C.E. to first century C.E., feature many of the texts Jewish and Christian communities would come to think of as biblical, plus many other books that never made it into what would come to be called the Hebrew Bible. Various clues in the Dead Sea Scrolls (use of special scripts or frequent citations and interpretations) reveal that these writings were special to the community. But the Dead Sea Scrolls reflect also different versions of sacred writings. Also challenging to our attempts to reconstruct "a Bible" for this community is that multiple scrolls, the medium used by the community for writing, could not be secured in a single larger book with cover and bindings to "fix" the contents in a certain order. The Dead Sea Scrolls provide us with much important information about authoritative religious writings, but don't provide "the Bible" (if by that we have in mind the Bible on our coffee tables) of early Jews.

The Septuagint

One indication that a text was valued is its translation into another language. Beginning in the sixth century B.C.E., some religious texts composed in Hebrew were translated into Aramaic, the vernacular language of the Persian Empire that came to rule over Israel after the Babylonians. Moreover, since many people in the Mediterranean world were Greek speakers, including Jews living outside the land of Israel, there was also a need for religious texts to be translated into Greek.

An ancient text called *The Letter of Aristeas* recounts Egyptian interest in a Greek translation of the Torah. It is unclear, however, whether "Torah" refers here to the first five books of the Bible or whether it more literally meant "the instruction" for the community in general. This legendary story, set in third century B.C.E. Alexandria, Egypt, describes the translation of the Torah by seventy-two scribes, six from each of the twelve tribes of Israel. According to Philo (a first century B.C.E./C.E. Jewish philosopher), all seventy-two translators, though working separately, arrived at the same translation of the Torah—a miracle! This story signaled to the early Jewish, Greek-speaking community that the Divine was involved in the whole enterprise, a divine stamp of approval.

The Greek translation of the Torah was called the Septuagint (or "the 70") after the seventy-two translators. Sometimes it is just called the "LXX"—the Roman numeral for "70" that recalls the story of the scribes. Nowadays, the Septuagint is typically the designation given to Greek translations of many Hebrew Scriptures. It includes the Tanak along with many books not preserved by later Jews as sacred, although in antiquity some Jews did view them that way. These texts—with names like Judith, Ben Sira, and 1 Maccabees—were inherited by and preserved in the Old Testaments of Christians who were the ancestors to Roman Catholics and Orthodox Christians.

While the birth of the Jewish Bible is shrouded in mystery, scholars have more to say about its development after the Common Era. Scholars differ on the matter of when and where the rabbis (Jewish teachers) settled upon a fixed and/or closed collection of writings that came to be called the Tanak, but see the process being settled during late antiquity (sometime between second and seventh centuries C.E.). Since the late 1800s, the notion prevailed of a council at the town of Yavneh in Israel held at the end of the first century. Supposedly, at this council, rabbis determined which books would be authoritative for the Jewish community, which had just reassembled following the destruction of the Temple in 70 C.E. Over the last forty or so years, scholars have challenged the idea of a council at Yavneh, in light of a lack of evidence. In any event, by probably the second century, the principal books of what would be the Tanak were collected and held a special authority over other books.

The formation of the New Testament

Christianity began in Judaism and thus received its "Scripture" from Judaism. Several New Testament writers refer to "the Law and the Prophets" or the "Scriptures." "Law" in Greek, the language of the New Testament, was used to translate the Hebrew word "Torah" ("instruction" or "teaching"). Therefore, the Scripture (or anachronistically, one might say "the Bible") of the earliest Christians appears to have been "the Torah and the Prophets," with scattered other texts from the Tanak, such as the Psalms.

Interestingly, Christians also regarded as Scripture other books associated with Israel (like the writings of Enoch) that would not be included in the Tanak (see Jude 1:14–15). But, since there was no New Testament as such in the time of Jesus and the first generations of Christians, the Scripture of early Christians was *not* the New Testament.

Since Christianity flourished in lands outside of Israel that utilized Greek as a common or widely used language, Christians inherited the Septuagint, the Greek translation of Jewish religious texts. The writings of Christians that concern Jesus, Jesus's first followers, and the emergence of the early church—for example, letters to churches written by Paul and the four gospels (Matthew, Mark, Luke, and John)—were composed and transmitted in Greek as well. An important theme they explore is Jesus's death and resurrection, and to a lesser extent, Jesus's ministry.

With the exception of the letters of Paul that were early (the majority are typically dated toward the middle of the first century C.E.), the New Testament writings are products of second and third generations of Christians, peoples of diverse cultural settings that included Asia Minor (modern-day Turkey) and Rome. These books and additional letters (some attributed to Paul) were mostly produced between the mid-first and early part of the second century C.E. They reflect diverse perspectives, theological needs, and aims of early Christians and teach us much about the history of early Christianity.

The writers of the four gospels (and the visionary who was responsible for the Book of Revelation) did not set out to write "history books" but to tell about the meaning of history, as these authors understood it. The authors of letters and homilies (like the "Epistle" to the Hebrews) addressed particular individuals, "congregations," or communities of early Christians, giving them religious guidance specially tailored to their own situations.

With Christianity's spread throughout the Mediterranean world, various communities came to cherish and preserve certain texts about Jesus. Communities in diverse places of the ancient world were introduced to the Christian message by different Christian leaders, who handed on different texts, traditions, and theologies. As writings amassed and circulated in the late first century and then second century, Christians encountered the writings of other communities. Sometimes they enthusiastically received these texts, but on occasion they disputed these writings.

Diverse books for diverse Christians

Even the writings that came to make up the New Testament, as well as other texts, tell of the divisions among early Christian communities. By the mid-second century, there is evidence of Christians openly debating which Christian writings are to be preferred and prohibited. For example, Marcion, a very influential Christian of the second century, argued that Christians should not read the Tanak or Old Testament. Instead, he said, they should read only a version of the Gospel of Luke and some of the writings of Paul because Marcion thought the God of the Hebrew Bible was different from the God of Jesus. In the same century, Irenaeus, the bishop of Lyons, made the case for Christians reading the Jewish Scriptures (unlike Marcion), four gospels (Matthew, Mark, Luke, and John), Acts of the Apostles, and the letters of Paul. But he condemned other books he considered unorthodox.

Amid such disputes, Christians especially in the third and fourth centuries C.E. became aware of one another's scriptural preferences. Remnants of these debates help us to understand how the formation of Christian Bible was a lengthy process. There are examples of lists, like that of the church historian Eusebius (ca. 300), which speak of writings that most Christians in the ancient world were accepting as authoritative, others that were disputed, and some writings that were utterly rejected. The festal letter of Athanasius, Bishop of Alexandria, also contains a list of the sacred texts Christians should read. In this letter dated to 367 C.E., Athanasius is unequivocal—he asserts the very texts Christians should read and proscribes (forbids) other texts he deems heretical. The contents of the contemporary Protestant Bible are quite close to what Athanasius includes, but not exact (e.g., he excludes Esther). Athanasius uses a form of the Greek word "canon" in his letter. While the term literally means "a measuring stick," in this context it refers to Athanasius's assessment of writings as authoritative. In modern usage, "canon" refers to a definitive collection of authoritative writings in a religious context; that collection would be fixed and closed (no writings would be added or subtracted).

Another source of information on Christian views of authoritative writings are from late antique Bibles themselves! Christians took advantage of the codex (a book with binding) that became a common form for communicating literature and bound together numerous texts they considered authoritative, including writings of the Old Testament and New Testament. Interestingly, while the contents of these Bible from the fourth century resemble to some extent our contemporary Christian Bibles, in other ways the contents diverge, featuring a number of early Christian writings that most Christians today do not know as Scripture. These examples demonstrate how an emerging collection of authoritative texts congealed for Christians through the second to the fourth centuries. Some might argue that by the second or third century, the broad outlines of the Christian Bible were in place. At the same time, these instances drive home the point that Christian Bibles developed in communities as the result of discussions about which texts reflected proper ("orthodox") and common or widespread ("catholic") beliefs about Jesus. Moreover, these ancient witnesses demonstrate that the Christian Bible developed slowly, not overnight, as the result of a gradual process. Deliberations over the contents of the Christian Bible took place over centuries.

Christian Bibles of later times

In addition to the writings of the New Testament, early Christians used the Septuagint, the Greek translation of the Hebrew Bible, as well as some additional Jewish writings as their Old Testament. As the Christian Bible emerged with a common core of texts, the greater collection was translated into other languages like ancient Ethiopic or Syriac. Jerome, the famous fourth-century saint and theologian, desired to make a fresh translation of the Old Testament from Hebrew manuscripts of the Tanak into Latin for the Roman Catholic Church, an emerging principal church in late antiquity, with the Bishop of Rome (now more commonly known as the Pope) as its leader. While Jerome was hesitant to include the writings not found in the Tanak (like 1 Maccabees), these writings remained part of the Old Testament for Roman Catholics even while the Latin translation of the Christian Bible was the preferred translation.

With leadership rooted in the Eastern part of Europe, Orthodox Christians continued to use the Septuagint and had a rather flexible approach to the contents of the Old Testament. In time, different regional branches of the Orthodox Church, like the Russian Orthodox Church and the Ethiopian Orthodox Church, would come to include even more writings in their Old Testament, and Orthodox Christianity permitted translation of the Greek Old Testament into the vernacular of different communities.

Discussions around the Bible became particularly heated around the time of the fifteenth to sixteenth centuries, though, with the German theologian Martin Luther. Luther set out to reform the Roman Catholic Church and one of his initiatives was translating the Bible from Latin into the language of the land. Luther valued Scripture over Church tradition and looked upon the Bible of the Jewish community as having an earlier or from his vantage more authentic collection of sacred texts. For this reason, he excluded from his Bible the additional writings from the Septuagint like Judith, Tobit, and so on.

As a result, the Roman Catholic Church called a meeting—the Council of Trent—and declared that contrary to Luther's view, the additional writings (which Christians took initially from the Septuagint) were authoritative Scripture! For Roman Catholics, these additional texts are "deuterocanonical" (secondarily canonical), a status which acknowledges that the books were received into the tradition at a later time, but are authoritative and canonical nonetheless.

Conclusion

This brief history takes us to the present. Bibles are collections of books that preserve the sacred stories of ancient Jews and Christians. There are many Bibles and Bibles evolved from individual writings to collections that were products of complex histories. And as Eugene Boring notes, "No text in the Bible speaks about the Bible as a whole. The idea that the canonical collection of

Scripture texts is in some sense the Word of God is a construction of postbiblical theology" (2012, 706). Still, if you were to ask a religious Jew or Christian today "What is the Bible?," they would likely have a shorter and very different answer from the one I've just given.

For many Jews and Christians today their Bible is the Word of God, writings inspired by (infused with) the Divine, or a repository of life-giving and timeless wisdom. For religious Jews and Christians—scholars, clergy (rabbis, priests, and ministers), and laypeople alike—the Bible as a book is sacred turf. It preserves a community's story and self-identity and tells of God's relationship with and wishes for humankind. The Bible speaks to people about the challenges of life and suffering and theological responses to these. It speaks to the deepest existential crises while also offering consolation, hope sometimes obscured by the day-to-day doldrums and worries. How do I know this? As a biblical scholar trained in both the secular academy and institutions with religious affiliations and as a biblical scholar mentored by and appreciative of colleagues from diverse backgrounds, I know that the value of the Bible for many extends beyond the light it sheds on history or cultural artifacts.

At the same time, for many communities the Bible has a checkered past. To paraphrase the feminist scholar Phyllis Trible, the Bible is a book of blessings and curses (Trible 2006, 52). As the other chapters in the volume have shown, the Bible is a complicated work, and complications extend to matters of interpretation among communities. Aware of these complications, thoughtful readers of Scripture do not strain common sense in their approach to reading sacred texts. Readers and religious communities are mindful of historical contexts and cultural assumptions that inform the various writings. They pay attention to the literary genre of the different texts that make up a Bible. They also come to know themselves better as readers of sacred texts; that is, in addition to knowing how their own communities value and read the Bible, they know the lens through which they see the world, and consider how it impacts their own reading of the Bible.

Being aware of the fact that there are many Bibles may help one to be a better dialogue partner in public debate and discourse, where religion and politics are involved. Realizing that the Bible did not just "fall from the sky" one day but is the result of long processes involving communities might also suggest to the ardent and zealous that religion is a complex phenomenon. The Bible is very much a community's (communities') book and belongs to each community, preserving sacred stories, histories, and views of God. This reality does not diminish the worth of the Bible. On the contrary, this aspect of the Bible ties it to the human family, to us all, as a timely, timeless, and often challenging collection of books.

Works Cited

Boring, M. Eugene. *An Introduction to the New Testament: History, Literature, Theology*. Louisville: Westminster John Knox, 2012.

Bowley, James. "Bible." In *The Oxford Encyclopedia of the Books of the Bible*, edited by M.D. Coogan. Vol. 1, 73–84. Oxford: Oxford University Press, 2011.

Lim, Timothy H. *The Formation of the Jewish Canon*. New Haven: Yale University, 2013.

Stuckenbruck, Loren. "Apocrypha and Pseudepigrapha." In *Eerdmans Dictionary of Early Judaism*, edited by J.J. Collins and D.C. Harlow, 143–162. Grand Rapids: Eerdmans, 2010.

Trible, Phyllis. "Wrestling with Scripture." *Biblical Archaeology Review* 32 (2006): 52.

Ulrich, Eugene. *The Dead Sea Scrolls and the Origins of the Bible*. Grand Rapids: Eerdmans, 1999.

Ulrich, Eugene. "The Jewish Scriptures: Texts, Versions, Canons." In *Eerdmans Dictionary of Early Judaism*, edited by J.J. Collins and D.C. Harlow, 97–119. Grand Rapids: Eerdmans, 2010.

13

Compromise as a Biblical Value

John F. Kutsko

Partisanship and absolutism abound in politics. While the 2016 U.S. presidential campaign may have appeared to be the high-water mark of divisiveness, we have seen a string of years with gridlock and the odds seem stacked against change.

In a 2012 opinion piece, Senator Joseph Lieberman described the two previous years as "two of the most uncompromising, unproductive years in our history." The title of his article, "Unlocking Congress Means Compromise," suggested compromise was the answer. He advised, "It's time to govern. And that means it is also time to compromise. I don't mean it is necessary to compromise principle, but it is necessary to understand that in a legislative body as diverse as Congress, if members demand 100 percent of what they prefer before voting for legislation, we will end up with zero legislation and worsening problems" (Lieberman 2012).

Senator Lieberman's advice went unheeded. In October 2013, the U.S. Federal Government shut down over the inability of Congress to compromise on a budget. The sixteen-day government shutdown was the third longest in U.S. history, with a significant cost to the economy (Kirell 2013; Mathews Burwell 2013). Undeterred, brinksmanship in 2014 took the Federal Government again to the eleventh hour before passing a budget for 2015 (Bradner et al. 2014). When campaigning for his Senate seat in 2012, candidate Ted Cruz ran on a promise he would not compromise: "We need to draw a line in the sand....If you're looking for an established moderate who will go to Washington and work across the aisle and compromise...I'm not the guy" (Evans 2012). True to his word, in both 2013 and 2014, Senator Ted Cruz led the initiatives to prevent passage of compromise budgets.

Passionate political, social, and religious debate regards compromise as a bad thing. It suggests one has given in, given up, conceded, and accommodated. Someone who compromises is wishy-washy. He has weakened his principles or she has lowered her standards. We have come to think of compromise in terms of surrendering our values, settling for less, getting the short end of the stick, losing, or even losing our way. We respect those people who do not compromise their principles.

The Bible, too, seems like an unlikely place to find compromise. Religion in general and the Bible in particular are often seen as undergirding rigid and inflexible positions, fueling conflict in our history books, and violence in our news reports (Hitchens 2007; Avalos 2005). To many people's way of thinking, the Bible is where we should find lessons that teach us not to compromise.

We are more likely to hear someone using the Bible to support racism, sexism, Islamophobia, homophobia, even capitalism, rather than social justice, community service, or love. A 2014 report noted that Nigeria's so-called whisper campaign to round up gay men used churches and mosques to help. The BBC reporter Will Ross said, "Everybody quoted the Bible or quoted the Koran" (Hills 2014). Those who were rounded up faced the death penalty if convicted, which in biblical fashion included stoning.

Religious and political authorities today sometimes choose proof texts to support their causes in myopic, polarizing, and selective fashions (Levinson 2006, 1853–1854). As we have seen in the preceding chapters of this book, this is done for all types of issues. The tone of debates is often presumed by the loaded expressions used for them, such as "creation science," "the biblical definition of marriage," "pro-life," or "family values." In the process, the Bible itself is assumed to be monolithic and one sided, with little complexity. This reinforces the perception that the Bible teaches us to be uncompromising.

So the last thing we think about when we look to religion is compromise. As with political parties, we may think of religion as drawing boundaries, building walls, and smiting our enemy. Religion connotes ideological positions that separate people and communities rather than ones that build bridges and join communities. Too often, religion breeds a self-assurance that we have the answer and that God is on our side. Indeed, a book on *The Bible in Political Debate* seems all summed up by the sage advice, "Never discuss religion and politics in polite company."

Nevertheless, I would argue that a large part of the Bible—the Hebrew Bible or Old Testament—practices compromise. It does it for a purpose surprisingly similar to our own twenty-first-century context, namely, to maintain community in the midst of diversity. Whether or not the world needs religion, it needs compromise, and in this the Bible has a lesson for us.

Compromise in the first five books of the Bible

The principle of compromise that I see in the Hebrew Bible is embedded in the process of its literary composition. Biblical scholarship of the type begun in the Enlightenment uncovers this dynamic. Scholars began focusing on the abrupt and inconsistent traits in biblical books and chapters: unique styles, distinct technical terminology, different religious viewpoints and perspectives existing alongside one another, contradictions and inconsistencies in details such as names and events, interruptions in the narrative, and repetitions and duplications of the same or similar stories that are mutually exclusive. These internal literary tensions became the starting points for scrutiny. To be sure, these internal inconsistencies were noticed by the earlier interpreters (e.g., Kugel 1997). However, more objective assumptions and reading methods in the Enlightenment period gave support to scholars who did not want to explain these problems away. They sought to answer them honestly with the tools used by scholars in other fields.

A major conclusion of this early scholarship was that the main effort to collect and edit texts in the Bible actively began in the sixth century B.C.E. This was when the kingdoms of ancient

Israel and Judah were attacked, the kings deposed, and many of the people were deported and sent into exile in Babylon. They became refugees. This mass exile continued through the period of the Persian Empire. The incentive to preserve past writings and histories should not surprise us. All the hopes and dreams of a nation were endangered. Social and religious identity was at risk of fading away. The community was scattered. The future was uncertain. It is natural in times of crisis to record our past to protect our present, and especially to explain our past in such a way as to give meaning to the future.

That past was not written by a single person from start to finish. Instead, the Bible came together through a complicated process with many hands in the mix. One of the contributions of modern biblical criticism to understanding part of that process is called the Documentary Hypothesis, a theory of how the first five books of the Hebrew Bible or Old Testament—Genesis, Exodus, Leviticus, Numbers, and Deuteronomy—were written. This set of books is called the Pentateuch or Torah (I will use the two terms interchangeably).

The Documentary Hypothesis is a method of reading a text that scholars call source criticism—that is, understanding the sources that make up a final document. The first person to write the most comprehensive presentation of the Documentary Hypothesis was the German scholar Julius Wellhausen, who published in 1878 what would later be called in English the *Prolegomena to the History of Israel* (1885). The central thesis of the Documentary Hypothesis is that the Pentateuch is the final product of four originally separate documents, each a *prolegomenon* (a preface or introduction). The documents were written centuries after the events narrated and then edited, one after the other, as sources were added. Wellhausen called the four documents J (for the German "Yahwist," since that source prefers the name Yahweh for God), E (for Elohist, that source's original name for God), D (for Deuteronomist, comprising especially the Book of Deuteronomy), and P (for the Priestly writer, due to its emphasis on priestly traditions). These four sources were not only independent but also parallel, covering the same range of people, places, and time in the biblical story, but written at different times.

Consider some of the glaring overlaps and inconsistencies in biblical texts that source criticism takes seriously. Right off the bat in the opening chapters of Genesis, the first book of the Bible, we find two creation stories that are not complementary. In Genesis 1 (the P source), plants are created before humans. In chapter 2 (the J source), it is the reverse. In chapter 1 (the P source), animals are also created before humans, while in chapter 2 (the J source) animals are created after the man and before the woman. The flood story in Genesis 6–9 is especially confusing, with two distinct stories (J and P) interwoven instead of just set side by side. For example, in those chapters the J source has Noah collect seven pairs of clean animals and one pair of unclean animals, while in the P source Noah is told to gather one pair of every species. In J, the rain falls for forty days, while in P the floods increase for 150 days. Throughout Genesis—the first book of the Pentateuch—the J source uses Yahweh for God's name, but the E source uses Elohim until God reveals the name Yahweh to Moses in Exodus—the second book of the Pentateuch. God's mountain is called Horeb (the E and D sources) and Sinai (the J and P sources). There are even two different sets of the Ten Commandments, one in Exodus 20 (the P source) and the other in Deuteronomy 5 (the D source). You can find a veritable library of academic books that describe and show these sources (e.g., Blenkinsopp 1992; Friedman 2003).

The Documentary Hypothesis was an attempt to explain and reconcile stylistic differences, inconsistencies, and repetitions that occur regularly throughout the Pentateuch. It showed that the Torah—the first five books of the Bible, was really four separate introductions intermingled.

Furthermore, Wellhausen did not just identify four sources of the Pentateuch. He suggested several more things. First, he put the four documents in a chronological order: J, E, D, and P, one after the other. Second, in telling those roughly parallel stories, he noted that each tells it subjectively from its perspective. Each is steeped in the values and concerns of the time it was written, not objectively portraying the events. Consequently, according to Wellhausen, these documents can be used to recover the history of Israel, century by century, by what each emphasizes. Reviewing these documents, Wellhausen concludes that Israel must have evolved from a more simple society to a more complex one. When placed in Wellhausen's chronological order, these stories reveal an evolutionary history of Israel's theologies and politics. Each document points to a phase or period of Israel's religion:

from a tribal religion that worshipped its God Yahweh with a spontaneous, natural religion; to a royal, national religion; to a religion dominated by the legal and ritual concerns of priests. The last stage was controlled by the final writers and editors, the priests who composed the Pentateuch in order to claim their social, political, and theological position in that society. History is written by the victor, the one who gets the last word.

Now consider Wellhausen's intellectual influences. Social and historical contexts shape our ideas in ways in which we might not even be aware or may simply take for granted—the sociology of knowledge. One philosophical influence on Wellhausen that helps explain his linear theory of history is self-evident. The foundation of evolutionary biology, Darwin's *On the Origin of Species*, was published in 1859. It influenced biblical studies, which applied an evolutionary model to history and theology (Knight 1983). The Pentateuch's sources, once identified for themes, were set in what was perceived to be an obvious development—from "primitive" and folksy religion (earliest) to law and order in a well-developed social class bureaucracy (latest).

The Documentary Hypothesis traced linear development from one party and theology at a time to the next. This view is similar to a species developing without alternative forms coexisting. The theory has been the dominant model for scholars.

In the last several decades, other biblical scholars have modified the Documentary Hypothesis in three directions. One direction sees an even more complex process with many more traditions, layers, and editorial hands involved in the writing of the Pentateuch. The differences were the result of having too many chefs in the kitchen. Another direction is to see more or less one author who composed this story, late in the exile, as a work of historical fiction with a strong political message. The differences are there because it needed a good editor or the author did not entertain modern notions of literary consistency. Both of these approaches still grapple with the nagging problem that began the theorizing: why did the community that preserved the Pentateuch tolerate contradictions that remain so very obvious? A third and more straightforward approach has developed recently that explains the inconsistencies and the historical context. For the community in exile the inconsistencies speak to an intentional process that had a rationale.

Before we look at the third approach, let's return to the issue of the Documentary Hypothesis's evolutionary premise. To be sure, we know the facts of evolutionary biology, but it is less applicable to ideology, theology, and politics—the world of ideas. Consider the world around us. Is there ever only one opinion on a religious issue at any one period of time? To be sure, it is reasonable that there were documents that made a single case or stated the position of a particular religious or political party in ancient Israel. Nevertheless, the existence of multiple, competing parties and positions in a community is not just reasonable but very likely and naturally expected. Certainly consensus building happens over time, but groups of people within a community maintain different ideas and positions alongside each other and are rarely completely silenced (Scott 1990). We know that cultures, ancient or modern, are not monolithic. Scholars have now come to see that parties and factions existed (Smith 1987). Religions coexisted in ancient Israel (Geller 2004). Judaisms and Christianities competed and also at times cooperated.

What if these groups in times of crisis drafted their history together, for the sake of the community's solidarity and survival? Strong cases have now been made to see two developments in the origin of the Pentateuch. The first recognizes the "existence of four continuous, coherent, originally independent documents that have been combined into a single story in the canonical text," and they were brought together at one time (Baden 2012, 214). The process does not presume a long editorial history, but a discrete and unique act of combining four traditions. The second is that the Pentateuch is a compromise document drafted during ancient Israel's exile (see Knoppers and Levinson 2007, 3–4; Römer 2009, 157; Fishbane 1985, 264–265). Leaders of the community composed a coalition constitution, "in which different narratives and legal collections were gathered together in an attempt to accommodate the different ideological points of view" (Römer 2008, 2).

The person or group overseeing the compilation did not seek to resolve inconsistencies because those inconsistencies and contradictions marked and highlighted the compromise. To have removed or smoothed the contradictions would have undermined the coalition's goal. The reason the compiler of this text was faithful to the content, the reason he or she did not create a nicely edited text, was to affirm each group that valued one of the sources as their special tradition. This combined text made a statement: "No one source, no one viewpoint, captures the entirety of the ancient Israelite religious experience....The competing voices preserved in the Pentateuch are, in fact, complementary, even as they disagree....The compilation of the Pentateuch sends a clear and resounding message about the diversity of ancient Israelite religious thought and the importance of giving equal voice to all of its disparate representations" (Baden 2012, 228).

Similar to how the Pentateuch gave equal weight to different views, the United States has historically tried to allow competing views to be heard and valued through its two-party system. Consequently, U.S. laws are usually compromises with language from both sides included in order to reach consensus. We see this dynamic, too, when we look back to the formative and messy business of drafting the U.S. Constitution at the Constitutional Convention of 1787 (Stewart 2008). Indeed, the U.S. Constitution is called "a bundle of compromises" (Farrand 1913, 201). This is the strength of the democratic system in diverse societies (Crick 2013). Additionally, the ability to compromise was the dominant trait of the most routinely admired U.S. President, Abraham Lincoln (Goodwin 2006).

Like the U.S. Constitution, the making of the first five books of the Bible was a community process. It involved multiple political and religious factions collaborating to form a coalition which maintained the community. Those involved sought to unify the people in the wake of national disaster and exile. Compromise was how they did it. The differences were left so that the resulting text was acceptable to multiple groups with competing convictions and principles. Each group needed to see in the text its own distinctive language and ideas. It was not an accident, the result of incompetence, or premodern literary sensibilities. The differences were foregrounded and intentional—they were markers of compromise. The Pentateuch is the Bible's constitutional compromise.

What if we acknowledged this as an example of a biblical value? As one scholar observed, "In the American context, the perception of religion in public discourse, whether from the right or from the left, tends to be one that sees the Bible in quite monolithic terms, as hierarchical and dogmatic, rather than as fostering critical thought and public debate" (Levinson 2008, xvi). In any society, there are legitimately diverse opinions on complex issues. The fact that the persons who compiled the Torah maintained views from distinct social groups is a model then and now for an intellectually and culturally rich society. It also requires now an intellectually active reading of the Bible that does not seek homogenous and simplistic answers.

A major part of the Bible—the first five books of both the Jewish and Christian canons—was composed in a way that emphasizes the need to band together, to find common cause, to see more in similarities than in differences. It teaches a model of unity, in spite of differences, as a core principle—a religious principle for establishing community.

Diversity here, there, and everywhere in the Bible

An important contribution of modern scholarship has been its honest recognition of diversity, multiple voices, and views where earlier we had seen homogeneity and uniformity. Before the rise of modern biblical scholarship, and for largely religious reasons, the Bible was often reduced to a theological narrative that ran unabated through the text. The Bible was read as a harmonious story line, one that developed book by book. The reality is far more complex (Hayes 2011, 25–38). We might find a helpful analogy in Mikhail Bakhtin's observation of "polyphony" in the novels of Fyodor Dostoevsky. Polyphony recognizes that many "conflicting ideological positions are given a voice and set in play both between and within individual speaking subjects, without being placed and judged by an authoritative authorial voice" (Lodge 1990, 86; Newsom 1996). In the Bible, we see that art does imitate life.

We do not even have to read in between the lines, as it were, to see the polyphony of the Pentateuch in other places in the Bible. What might the collection of books together tell us about the community that collected them as a sacred text, as a constitutional document? If you do not try to read uniformity into the canon of the Bible, if you are open to the polyphony of the text, you'll see many dialogues and disagreements between entire books. For example, you'll find an argument for pacifism in Daniel and militant self-defense in

Esther; divine judgment in Joel and divine mercy in Jonah; and ethnic exclusivity in Ezra and Nehemiah, but ethnic inclusivity in Ruth. The New Testament has four Gospels with their own set of frequently contradictory narratives. Multiple views coexist in all healthy communities.

As with the formation of the Pentateuch, when multiple religious parties collaborated over a coalition constitution, books presenting diametrically opposed views were accepted into the canon together. The Bible includes alternative positions and viewpoints, and recognizes intense debate after the exile that would have continued for centuries. A religious community was united, not divided, by integrating multiple views. This tradition modeled the principle that the whole is greater than the sum of its parts. To put a premium on community, one must practice compromise.

The Bible does not give simple answers to the problem of good and evil, mercy versus justice, or friend versus foe. Different answers resonate with different parts of the community at different times (Eccl. 3). We should marvel at the Bible's unresolved polyphony of voices. We might see it as a model for community that an ancient text would include very different approaches to fundamental human and national questions. Such an attitude in a community required constant negotiation and compromise, indicative of viewing each other with respect. Compromise was a guiding principle because community was a primary goal. The Torah might have started with the preamble, "We the people, in order to form a more perfect union..."

When we constrain the Bible to give simple answers rather than use it as a model for making meaning, we undermine its influence, value, and even authority. It leads to extremism and polarization. We have seen candidates for political office who have characterized whole nations, religions, and ethnicities as criminals and extremists, without seeing the extremism in the position itself. There are serious consequences to our political systems and civil discourse when compromise gives way to extremism (Ryan 2016). The Pew Research Center's Religion and Public Life Project released a report showing that "the share of countries with a high or very high level of social hostilities involving religion reached a six-year peak in 2012" (Pew 2014). Religious social hostility, which included "abuse of religious minorities by private individuals or groups in society for acts perceived as offensive or threatening to the majority faith," was reported in 47 percent of countries in 2012, up from 24 percent in 2007. Religious hostility doubled in five years. Religion is a factor that indisputably influences our politics (Sacks 2003) and that influence is only expected to rise (Pew 2015). Sage advice should be to "always discuss religion and politics in civil society."

In our daily lives, we coexist with people of different and layered views. Ideas too easily labeled conservative or liberal, reactionary or progressive, are bookends to real-life complexity that exists along a spectrum. They rarely fit in neat little boxes or bodies. Uniformity is not just the opposite of diversity, it is also unrealistic in community.

Pluralism, multiculturalism, and globalization require compromise in our local neighborhoods and in our global villages. Make of it what you want, compromise is a core principle in the Bible—a text that can teach us urgent lessons to foster peace and understanding in our complex and diverse communities.

Works Cited

Avalos, Hector. *Fighting Words: The Origins of Religious Violence.* Amherst, NY: Prometheus Books, 2005.

Baden, Joel S. *The Composition of the Pentateuch: Renewing the Documentary Hypothesis.* New Haven: Yale University Press, 2012.

Blenkinsopp, Joseph. *The Pentateuch: An Introduction to the First Five Books of the Bible.* New York: Doubleday, 1992.

Bradner, Eric, Barrett, Ted and Levy, Adam. "Senate Sends Spending Bill to Obama, Avoiding Government Shutdown." *CNN.* December 13, 2014.

Crick, Bernard. *In Defence of Politics*, 5th edn. London: Bloomsbury Academic, 2013.

Evans, Glenn. "U.S. Senate Candidate Ted Cruz: No Compromising." *The Longview News Journal.* May 18, 2012.

Farrand, Max. *The Framing of the Constitution of the United States.* New Haven: Yale University Press, 1913.

Fishbane, Michael. *Biblical Interpretation in Ancient Israel.* Oxford: Clarendon Press, 1985.

Friedman, Richard Elliott. *The Bible with Sources Revealed.* San Francisco: HarperCollins, 2003.

Geller, Stephen, "The Religion of the Bible." In *The Jewish Study Bible: Jewish Publication Society Tanakh Translation*, edited by Adele Berlin, Marc Zvi Brettler and Michael Fishbane, 2021–2040. Oxford: Oxford University Press, 2004.

Goodwin, Doris Kearns. *Team of Rivals: The Political Genius of Abraham Lincoln*. New York: Simon & Schuster, 2006.

Hayes, Christine Elizabeth. *The Emergence of Judaism: Classical Traditions in Contemporary Perspective*. Minneapolis: Fortress Press, 2011.

Hills, Carol (producer). "Local Authorities Use a Whisper Campaign to Round Up Gay Men in Northern Nigeria." *PRI*. February 07, 2014.

Hitchens, Christopher. *God Is Not Great: How Religion Poisons Everything*. New York: Hachette, 2007.

Kirell, Andrew. "A Brief History of the 2013 Government Shutdown." *Mediaite*. October 17, 2013.

Knight, Douglas A. (ed.). *Julius Wellhausen and His Prolegomena to the History of Israel. Semeia* 25. Chico, CA: Scholars Press, 1983.

Knoppers, Gary N. and Levinson, Bernard M. "How, When, Where, and Why Did the Pentateuch Become the Torah?" In *The Pentateuch as Torah: New Models for Understanding Its Promulgation and Acceptance*, edited by Bernard M. Levinson and Gary Knoppers, 1–19. Winona Lake, IN: Eisenbrauns, 2007.

Kugel, James L. *The Bible as It Was*. Cambridge, MA: Harvard University Press, 1997.

Levinson, Bernard. "The First Constitution: Rethinking the Origins of Rule of Law and Separation of Powers in Light of Deuteronomy." *Cardozo Law Review* 27:4 (2006): 1853–1888.

Levinson, Bernard. *Legal Revision and Religious Renewal in Ancient Israel*. Cambridge: Cambridge University Press, 2008.

Lieberman, Joe. "Unlocking Congress Means Compromise." *The Hartford Courant*. November 16, 2012.

Lodge, David. *After Bakhtin: Essays on Fiction and Criticism*. New York: Routledge, 1990.

Mathews Burwell, Sylvia. "Impacts and Costs of the October 2013 Federal Government Shutdown." Whitehouse.gov. November 7, 2013. https://www.whitehouse.gov/blog/2013/11/07/impacts-and-costs -government-shutdown (accessed January 11, 2016).

Newsom, Carol A. "Bakhtin, the Bible, and Dialogic Truth." *The Journal of Religion* 76:2 (1996): 290–306.

Pew Research Center. "Religious Hostilities Reach Six-Year High." January 14, 2014. http://www.pewforum.org/2014/01/14/religious -hostilities-reach-six-year-high/(accessed February 10, 2016).

Pew Research Center. "The Future of World Religions: Population Growth Projections, 2010–2050." April 2, 2015. http://www .pewforum.org/files/2015/04/02/religious-projections-2010-2050/ (accessed April 10, 2015).

Römer, Thomas. "The Exodus Narrative According to the Priestly Document." In *The Strata of the Priestly Writings: Contemporary*

Debate and Future Directions, edited by Sarah Shectman and Joel S. Baden, 157–170. Zürich: Theologischer Verlag, 2009.

Römer, Thomas. "Moses Outside the Torah and the Construction of a Diaspora Identity." *Journal of Hebrew Scriptures* 8 (2008): 2–12.

Ryan, Timothy J. "No Compromise: Political Consequences of Moralized Attitudes." *American Journal of Political Science* 60 (2016): 1–15.

Sacks, Jonathan. *The Dignity of Difference: How to Avoid the Clash of Civilizations*, 2nd edn. London: Bloomsbury Academic, 2003.

Scott, James C. *Domination and the Arts of Resistance: Hidden Transcripts*. New Haven: Yale University Press, 1990.

Smith, Morton. *Palestinian Parties and Politics That Shaped the Old Testament*, 2nd edn. London: SCM, 1987.

Stewart, David O. *The Summer of 1787: The Men Who Invented the Constitution*. New York: Simon & Schuster, 2008.

NOTES

Introduction

1   An important exception to note is Chancey et al. (2014), which is an excellent contribution to examining the role of the Bible in the public arena.

Chapter 1

1   All autobiographical reflections are those of Jack Levison.
2   When California enacted similar laws in 1968, legal abortions rose from 5,000 in 1968 to over 100,000 in 1972 (Williams 2011).
3   When Carter subsequently informed Fleming of his intention to appoint a co-chair to ease tensions, she resigned.
4   Every other topic mentioned in the platform, including paperwork reduction, received more discussion than families.

Chapter 7

1   My thanks to John Burgess for sharing his translation of "Prepodobnomuchenitsa Mariia (Tseitlin)" (Burgess 2006, 24).
2   The translation in this case and what follows is from the New Revised Standard Version.

Printed in the USA
CPSIA information can be obtained
at www.ICGtesting.com
LVHW020525240124
769578LV00003B/121